The Tactical Pistol

Advanced Gunfighting Concepts and Techniques

Gabriel Suarez
foreword by Jeff Cooper

PALADIN PRESS
BOULDER, COLORADO

Dedicated, as all first books should be, to my parents, who risked everything to take their children from the clutches of communism and bring them to the New World so that we might grow up as free men . . . so that we might grow up as Americans.

The Tactical Pistol:
Advanced Gunfighting Concepts and Techniques
by Gabriel Suarez

Copyright © 1996 by Gabriel Suarez

ISBN 0-87364-864-1
Printed in the United States of America

Published by Paladin Press, a division of
Paladin Enterprises, Inc., P.O. Box 1307,
Boulder, Colorado 80306, USA.
(303) 443-7250

Direct inquiries and/or orders to the above address.

Contents

Foreword

To be a master of pistolcraft, it is not enough to be a good shot, though that is certainly a part of the total capacity. Mastery of marksmanship is an essential element of the proper mind-set which is necessary for success in lethal combat, but the proper mind-set, which enables one to triumph in a deadly encounter, is nearly impossible to inculcate in advance. Only the man who has been there—"seen the elephant"—really knows if he can employ the principles of marksmanship when he is faced with a deadly enemy who is trying to kill him. Thus it is that Gabriel Suarez is particularly well-qualified to write the book that you are about to read, because he is not only a fine shot, as he has demonstrated to me several times at Old Gunsite, but he has also shown that he can employ his high order of skill when the chips are down. Gabe has seen success in combat several times in our ongoing war against crime, and serving as he does as a full-time police officer in Southern California, the chances are that he will do so again before he chooses to retire.

In recruiting instructors for Old Gunsite, I used to look for five elementary qualifications. The first was marksmanship. The teacher had to be able to do anything he asks his students to do, and do it easily and without apparent effort. After that, the teacher must possess a genuine desire to impart. I have known several people who were wonderful shots but did not want anybody else to be. A really good instructor must be more interested in the excellence of his students than of his own. Third, the superior instructor must have what is known in the military as "command presence," because he must exert unquestioned authority over people who are not under his command. He must command by his posture, attitude, voice, and general air of confidence, without relying upon rank. Fourth, the range instructor must comport himself as a gentleman. In this scruffy age, it is sometimes difficult to find a man who can do that, but we still make the effort. But finally, and most important, the Doctor of Marksmanship must have been in combat, having been shot at and shot back successfully. Otherwise, when he tells students what they must do, he will have no authority for his statement. He must be able to say, "I know you can do this because I have been there and I have done it."

In all of these foregoing characteristics, Gabriel Suarez is eminently qualified. I can think of no one better able to tell you how it is done.

I suggest you pay particularly close attention to what Gabe has to say about this curious modern phenomenon called "Post Operational Trauma," or POT for short. People certainly are not the same, and one will not respond to critical stress the same as another, but the idea that it will be normal for a combatant to go to pieces after he has won a fight is ridiculous. If that were true, the human race would never have advanced beyond the baboon stage. When you win a fight, you are not upset. On the contrary, you are pleased and proud. Gabe can tell you about this from personal experience, and I can second the motion.

Gabriel Suarez is a Master *Pistolero*. If you take his teachings to heart and practice what he preaches, your reward will be a feeling of serenity and peace of mind which will enhance the rest of your life.

This is the law.
The purpose of fighting is to win.
There is no possible victory in defense.
The sword is more important than the shield
and skill is more important than either.
The final weapon is the brain.
All else is supplemental.

John Steinbeck

Preface

The pistol has been part of the tactical "big picture" for more than 500 years, but only recently (historically speaking) has it truly arrived as an effective defensive weapon.

Three milestones in weapons development mark the history of the pistol as it is today. The first of these was Col. Samuel Colt's development of the repeating pistol. The second, facilitated by the invention of smokeless powder, was the self-loading pistol developed by John Moses Browning. The final step was not a technical one but rather a tactical one. This was the birth of the Modern Technique as established by Col. Jeff Cooper and his associates.

The pistol today is at its zenith as a reactive tool. It is a defensive weapon that is worn on the person in general anticipation of an unexpected fight. In this role it truly shines. The primary utility of the defensive pistol is its ease of carry, which allows around-the-clock protection. It will, theoretically, always be there when you need it.

The presence of the pistol alone, however, is not enough. The operator must have a firm understanding of marksmanship, gunhandling, and mind-set. These three equally important components make up what is called the "combat triad." Any shooting endeavor necessarily deals with marksmanship, but that should not be the only concern. The marksmanship problems presented in combat situations are not difficult, but even a master shooter will die if he does not manage his weapon adroitly under stress or if he is taken by surprise because he was not paying attention. Equally important is an understanding of the way fights develop and progress. No two gunfights are identical, but they all share patterns and similarities. Our training programs must take those dynamics into consideration or we will be fooling ourselves into believing we are ready to handle violence when it is offered to us.

My purpose in writing this book is to dispel the many myths and misconceptions prevalent about gunfighting by studying the dynamics of actual shootings and then organizing training concepts to accommodate real-world needs. I am not attempting to reinvent the wheel, but rather I am hoping to make it perform better under hazardous road conditions.

I do not consider this to be a master's text, but it certainly goes beyond the realm of the novice or beginning shooter. Such readers are admonished to proceed with caution, because attempting sophisticated shooting techniques without a thorough foundation in the basics will lead to failure. Several sources for basic instruction are listed in the bibliography. This work will be of greatest value to those already schooled in the subject who are seeking to become more "realistic." The information herein is presented to both the police officer and the righteous armed citizen, because not only can neither one succeed without the cooperation and assistance of the other, but their "battlefields" are really more similar than they realize.

The methods presented in this book are what I believe to be the best available. They were developed and successfully implemented by some of the greatest gunfighters on earth. They have all been tested in that crucible that some call "the dark place." I've been to that place. I know the sudden urgency that hostile gunfire can generate. I know the shrill exhilaration of chasing an armed adversary through the dark alleys of the urban jungle. I have been to the crime scenes in the wee hours of the morning, seen the results of being unprepared, and the tears and the blood of those victims whose last thoughts were that it could never happen to them. So read on! Learn, practice, and get ready to fight. I sincerely pray that this book will help light the way when you find yourself in "the dark place."

Gabriel Suarez
Los Angeles, 1995

Acknowledgments

No book is ever the work of one man, and this one is no exception. The following individuals have been of immense help in one form or another leading to the completion of this work.

I must thank, most of all, Col. Jeff Cooper, whose training at the Old Gunsite Ranch kept me alive long enough to get all of this down on paper, and whose assistance and advice on the book was invaluable.

Thanks to Chuck Taylor for training in his advanced combat shooting techniques and tactics.

Thanks to Dr. Ignatius (Naish) Piazza, president of Front Sight Firearms Training Institute, who provided the impetus and forum for much of my research.

Thanks to Brad Ackman, also of Front Sight Firearms Training Institute, for his thorough assistance with the manuscript.

Thanks to "X," trainer of warriors, and his shooters, who took time to assist with my research. Their duties require the anonymity of the shadows and preclude the naming of names. You know who you are!

Thanks to my partner Alfred Acosta for his assistance with the photographs—and for playing the "bad guy."

Last, but certainly not least, many thanks to my wife Cheryl for her assistance with the manuscript, the computer, and my spelling. I can never repay her understanding for those times when I was away "working," particularly for those times in the spring of '92 and the winter of '94 when she alone defended the homestead against the barbarians.

The *raison d'être* of the Armed Citizen

This book is primarily about fighting with pistols, yet it is also a guide for developing a certain way of thinking. Success in personal combat is more a matter of mind than of tools. This unique frame of mind is the "combat mind-set," and it begins by realizing that we live in a violent world. All you need to do to see that is to read the paper, watch the evening news, or venture out of your protected castles into the urban night. Oh yes, we live in a violent world and it shows every indication of becoming even more violent into the next century.

The only way to curb the violent crime infesting our nation, without sacrificing our free society, is the swift and terrible punishment of the criminal. It is unlikely that our kinder and gentler (really meaning softer and weaker) judicial system will take such a direction, in my lifetime at least. Until we decide to deal harshly with criminals, there will be no deterrent, and as long as there is no deterrent, criminals will continue with their activities. The next victim selected might be you!

What can we do about this? I have an idea. Armed, law-abiding citizens can make it very dangerous for the criminal to prey on society. You, the reader, must be the deterrent!

I believe we have the right—actually the moral duty—to resist the criminal oppressor. Quite simply, he who robs (insert your favorite heinous act here) and runs away, lives to rob another day.

There are those who advocate nonresistance. They would rather give up their car or wallet to "avoid trouble." I would ask them where they draw the line. What will they say when the thugs ask for their wife or kids, or their house, or their bank account, or even their nation? It is not an issue of losing material property. There is much more to it than that. We resist because free men and women resist. Free men are not slaves to oppressors or aggressors of any sort. So we fight not for our wallets (though they be empty) nor for our cars (though they be insured) but rather for our freedom. The author Robert Heinlein wrote, "The price of freedom is the willingness to do sudden battle anywhere, anytime, and with utter recklessness." That about says it all.

To resist you need the tools of resistance, which in our modern age are usually firearms. Foremost you need the will and the ability to use those tools at the required "moments of truth." Lack of will has caused more innocent deaths than lack of ability.

One notably poignant incident springs to mind. A man was set upon in his own home by three hoodlums intent on robbing him. The goons were not armed with firearms and were substantially smaller (physically) than their intended victim. The man, however, offered no resistance as they forced him to the floor and tied him up. He told them where the money and all the valuables were. Then they killed him in a particularly ugly way. The three were later captured and stood trial, but even the longest prison sentence will not reverse their deed.

The message is clear: this man could have easily trashed the three goons and lived to tell about it. But he lacked the will to do so and died without resistance.

A different story involves the owner of a jewelry store in what was once a "good part of town." The proprietor was a dealer in expensive jewelry and Rolex watches. One fine day he was robbed at gunpoint and, barely having lived through it, he promised himself that it would never happen again. He told me that he wasn't concerned about losing his property but rather did not want some thug having any control over him. He armed himself, practiced with his weapons, and cultivated his will. In the next few years he thwarted no less than three armed robberies with terminal results for the robbers.

The deciding issue for the two men in these stories was the will and capability to act with severity and ferocity when faced with violence. History clearly shows that such determined resistance yields the most favorable results. Those results are the protection of freedom, the preservation of life, and the defeat of the criminal in that very order. That resistance is empowered by will and expedited by the presence and proficient use of arms. That, in the end, is the *raison d'être* of the armed citizen.

Getting Your Mind Right

There are a number of evil people in our society who, for entirely selfish reasons, will take it upon themselves to bash your head in. Such things happen every day and are happening this very instant. The development of a combat attitude begins with the simple realization that the cartridge now sitting in the chamber of your pistol may be the very one you will need to save your life in the coming hour! Combat may come to anyone at anytime. Expect it.

The next evolution of this mind-set is the willingness to do something about this violence when it does come. It is not enough to be a competent marksman and to know that the "elephant" may lurk around the next corner. You must be *willing* to do something about it.

My own experiences and those of several dozen colleagues that I've spoken with bear witness that a proper mind-set is the key to winning a fight. The key is to know that there is going to be a fight *before* it starts.

The problem is that you cannot go through life "ready and willing," with hands poised over your pistols an eye-blink away from the killing stroke. You can't even anticipate specifi-

The cartridge now sitting in the chamber of your pistol may be the one you'll need in the next few seconds to defend your life!

cally when a fight will occur, although you can anticipate generally that it might. You need to develop a state of mind where the appearance of a sudden threat will not surprise you. When faced with a threat, you must not think, "My God, what is happening here?" but rather, "I knew this would happen and I am *ready* and *willing* to do something about it!" Instead of meeting a threat with astonishment, meet it with contempt.

Most human beings, however, are reluctant to visit harm on another person even when under attack. For example, as you sit reading this, you are emotionally and psychologically unprepared to kill another man. Even if you were attacked suddenly, it would take several precious seconds to realize what was really happening. The reaction most people have to sudden violence is disbelief. They can't seem to grasp the reality of the situation. Even after it is clear that it is truly life-or-death combat, they seem inclined to try to "bargain" their way out. They want to negotiate a way out of a non-negotiable situation. Such actions (actually inaction) will lead to disaster. A proper outlook negates this mental paralysis.

To ensure proper reactions, you need to develop an escalating state of alertness and subsequent readiness. This will help ensure appropriate reactions to any threat as well as protect against overreaction. The best way to develop this is through a study of the "color code of awareness." Here, certain colors are associated with escalating states of awareness. Unquestionably the most valuable lesson that I learned from Col. Jeff Cooper was the color code and the development of the subsequent combat mind-set. This little bit of knowledge saved my hide on at least a dozen occasions. It is with due credit and gratitude to the Colonel that I include it here.

Condition White

The first mental state is a state of unreadiness. It is characterized by the color white. You are in condition white when you are completely oblivious to your surroundings, such as when you are sleeping, engrossed in a good book, or daydreaming. Condition white is comfortable, and it is where your lazy mind will drift to if you allow it. Condition white comes from unfocused attention, actually inattention. If you are attacked while drifting in condition white, you can be killed easily. You cannot avoid condition white, and you lapse into it daily. You need to avoid it whenever you are away from home or around strangers and especially whenever you are under arms.

Condition Yellow

If condition white is relaxed inattentiveness, then the next level of readiness is relaxed attention. It is characterized by the color yellow. When you are in condition yellow you are aware of your surroundings. You know what is behind you (or, as fighter pilots say, you "check your six"). You notice the occupants of vehicles around you at traffic lights. You notice anyone whose actions might be keyed to yours or anyone that appears startled by your presence. Such things can be possible danger clues. Ninety-nine percent of the time they will be harmless, but you are ready for the time when they are not. You are careful not to give a stranger your hand or to take your eyes off him to give him the time from your wristwatch. You are alert and attentive. You realize that there is a very real possibility that you may have to fight for your life, but you don't know when or against whom. In other words, you know that you may have to shoot but you do not have a specific target.

Condition Orange

The next level of awareness is condition orange. Here you have noticed a possible specific problem and you begin developing a tactical plan. Now you realize that not only might you have to shoot, but you might have to shoot a particular individual. It is relatively easy to transition mentally from condition yellow to condition orange, but not from white to orange.

I recall a particular incident some years ago when my wife and I went out to do some Christmas shopping at the local mall. As we walked down the main building, I made eye contact with a particularly scruffy type as he walked past us. There was something about him that looked unusual. I had been in the police business for some time, and it was not uncommon to come across "clients" while off-duty now and then. I thought he might be one of those, although I did not recognize him. I was in condition yellow—relaxed, unspecified alert. We continued walking.

Moments later I looked over my shoulder to see where our friend had gone and saw that he was also looking over his shoulder at us. Hmmm. Unusual? Yes. A threat? Not yet. We turned a corner and began walking toward our destination about 50 yards away. I again looked over my shoulder, and what do you think I saw? Our friend had turned and was walking in our direction. "OK, this might be a problem," I thought. There was no overt threat, and his intentions could have been completely innocent. He was not viewed as a possible enemy . . . yet. I took my wife by the arm and we walked into an adjacent store. She immediately asked if I had seen the man that was following us. (She had been paying attention too!)

At that moment our scruffy friend walked into the same store and began looking around. He was not looking at merchandise but at the customers! Too much for coincidence, in my opinion. His actions were clearly keyed to ours. I shifted my state of readiness to condition orange—I had a possible target. If he had produced a weapon or made any aggressive act, I would have dropped him like a bad conversation!

I quickly analyzed my options. We had already tried avoidance without success. He had not actually done anything but look suspicious (which, as any policeman knows, is not against the law). His only transgression was to base his actions on what we were doing. By the rules of engagement we had to allow him to move first.

What followed was a very tense maneuvering around the store, with him pretending not to notice me at all. He looked like he wanted to get between me and my wife, but I would not let him. I was watching him carefully, and my planned response was set and ready to go if he offered any violence. After a few minutes he left the store, visibly flabbergasted, and melted into the crowd outside. We shifted back down into condition yellow.

After we mentioned the "suspicious guy" to the mall security officers, we concluded our shopping. On our way out we noticed the local police escorting our friend away in handcuffs. I asked the officer in charge what had happened. It seems he'd been "casing" the mall for unwary shoppers and tried to rob one of them at knife point! I wonder if he knows how close he came to the prison of no parole for bringing a knife to a gunfight.

Condition Red

Transition from condition orange to the next level is dependent on the actions of the bad guy. You reach condition red when you realize that a fight is now quite probable. You've made up your mind that the situation may warrant a lethal response, and all systems are GO! The pistol may be holstered, but it will probably be in hand, and a shot will be available in the blink of an eye. You are now actively looking for the cue that will trip your "mental trigger" and launch your terminal response.

This mental trigger is any aggressive action on the part of the enemy that justifies your use of deadly force. This trigger may be a weapon in the adversary's hand or anything that conveys that you are under attack. The mental trigger must be established in the mind long before the fight so that when the adversary gets the ball rolling, you will not need to debate the issue. Your response will be a conditioned response—instantaneous. Only certain preset checks—such as a perceived enemy identifying himself as an undercover police officer or realizing that the shadow with a gun is really a uniformed officer—will prevent your response.

This color code brings you progressively and justifiably closer to the level of deadly force with each escalation. Simultaneously, it decreases the possibility of overreaction to a perceived threat. If that threat is real, however, it decreases your reaction time and allows you to take care of business quickly and efficiently or avoid it completely.

When the fight has begun, you cannot let your mind drift or fix on irrelevant issues such as the danger you are in or what your peers will think. You need to focus all of your attention on the matter at hand. If you miss a shot, do not dwell on that. Neither do you consider the possibility that you *might* miss, nor the fact that you *might* be killed in the next few seconds. Neither seek to evaluate the past, nor anticipate the future. Rather, experience and concentrate on the moment as it is occurring. This means that you are focusing your concentration and attention on what you are doing *now*. Think like William Tell: "This shot right now is the only one that matters or will ever matter." You experience your actions as they are occurring in the present to the exclusion of all else. (Incidentally, the human mind under stress can only focus on one thing at a time. Focusing forcefully on your shooting will prevent the negative effects of terror and the subsequent panic that it leads to.)

After the last brass cartridge case has bounced on the reddening asphalt, you would think that the problem would be over. In essence the most important part of it is, since you are alive and your attacker is not. You've won, and that is eminently preferable to the dark alternative.

Many police writers, trainers, and psychologists do not let it go at that. They've given rise to all manner of disorders, complexes, and maladies that will allegedly pop up as residual effects of having successfully repelled boarders! You would think that such foolishness should be dismissed easily.

The problem is evident when you realize how impressionable the human mind is. Incredibly, many persons who choose to go about their business armed have not given the issue of actually having to kill another man much thought. They are honestly not sure about how they will feel. They are then told day after day from all sectors that they will feel terrible, have nightmares, and experience all manner of psychological problems if they win a fight. After a while—just like East German brainwashing victims—they begin to believe what they are told. So now we have an entire generation of armed citizens (and police) who expect to fall down in tears after they blast some raping, robbing, child-molesting, drug-addicted goblin to hell. They've been done a grave and horrible disservice. I don't doubt that someone somewhere had problems of this sort, but that neither means that it is acceptable nor inevitable!

No one can tell you with any certainty how you will feel after winning a fight. You can, however, begin to program attitudes that will help you prevail in the before and during phases. These same attitudes will tend to make you view the result of your victory more realistically.

Remember our discussion about how impressionable the human mind is? This very weakness can be used to your advantage. There is a very fine line (mentally speaking) between something you've experienced and something you've imagined. Here is the secret. You will tend to react before, during, and after a fight the way you've programmed yourself to act or the way you *expect* yourself to act! If you've trained properly and have programmed proper reactions in your mind, you will react that way. But it goes further than that.

You can also program the way to think! You can conduct mental rehearsals of every probability in your life where you might meet a fight. You solve those tactical problems in your mind's eye and picture yourself being cool under fire, shooting straight, and not being "bothered" by the result. You "see" that someone who would do you harm is an aberration condemned by his own actions. *You feel no remorse at his demise, because to do so is to mourn your own survival.*

Learn to control your thinking the same way you learn to control your shooting. This is not anything new. Many successful professional athletes use this method to control and prevent negative thoughts during play. Take a page from their book!

After the fight, there will probably be a sensation of relief followed by a sense of accomplishment and elation at being alive. This feeling will sometimes last for several days. There will be an overwhelming urge to tell your tale to anyone who will listen. Resist it! Seek instead to be as low profile as possible. There'll be those who will be horrified at what you've done regardless of your righteousness, legality, or necessity. Ignore them. Such people deserve no consideration and do not belong in your life. The press may include a report of your deed in their daily obfuscations. Be ready for such things. A study of how police investigate shooting incidents and a review of your particular legal position should have been seen to long before the fact in the preincident management phase so you'll know what to expect. I am not an attorney and I can give no formal advice on legal matters. Such things vary with the landscape, but you are well-advised to seek local advice on such issues.

Study your particular situation and develop a plan that covers tactical issues as well as any legal questions that may arise later. Before the fight, be alert, be ready, and be willing. During the fight, concentrate on solving the problem to the exclusion of all else (this usually means shooting well). After the fight, be pleased and proud of your performance, but exhibit a low-profile for the cameras, and do not listen to anyone who would tell you different—it is better to win than to lose. This may not sit well with the "kinder, gentler" crowd, but that is all there is to it.

Issues of Gun Safety

When asked about safety with firearms, the fearful man would say that all guns are dangerous. The tactical man would reply that indeed they are dangerous, because if they were not they would be useless! Firearms are really only tools, harmless and inert until touched by the hand of man. There are really no dangerous guns, but, as Heinlein says, only dangerous people.

Safety with firearms means that only the adversary (or the target on the firing range) is in danger of being shot. Absolutely no one and nothing else is in danger. Some people who are unfamiliar with martial activities may view the carrying of any loaded firearm as "dangerous." However, safety with that firearm is the responsibility of the user, not the observer.

Safety with anything is a mental process which must be learned and faithfully practiced to be effective. "Accidents" with firearms cannot be prevented with laws or gun locks or with guns too safe to be of any tactical value. Gun accidents are caused by inept and careless handling by people who lack the proper mind-set. Guns do not "go off" by them-

The "Golden Rule" of pistolcraft: **keep the finger off the trigger until the sights are on the target!**

selves; someone makes them go off. Weapons fired by mistake cause great embarrassment and sometimes tragedies. When this happens, it is often easier for the sinner to blame the instrument rather than admit his own incompetence and accept responsibility.

Accidental discharges are not "accidents" at all. They are caused by *negligence* and must always be called negligent discharges.

Part of the Modern Technique of the Pistol involves the understanding of gun safety. Colonel Cooper compressed the myriad of safety suggestions and rules into a total of four. They are clear, concise, and easy to remember.

Rule One: *All guns are always loaded.* We are much more careful with a gun that we know is loaded. That is as it should be. Guns are useless if they are not loaded. So always begin with the assumption that they *are* loaded. When handling the piece in an administrative manner, first check it to verify its condition and, if necessary, unload it. But always presume and expect that gun to be loaded.

Rule Two: *Never let the muzzle cover anything you are not willing to destroy.* This rule is applicable in administrative handling as well as in tactical duties. If someone points a weapon at you, it is implied that he is willing to destroy you. You are justified in taking offense at this. The excuse is usually the often-heard whine, "It's not loaded." He should be referred to rule one.

In some tactical situations, it is necessary to cover with the gun muzzle someone who is presumed, but not yet confirmed, to be the adversary. Doing so is not a violation of rule two. If a subject is acting in a manner that causes me to draw the pistol in the first place, or if I am searching an area for an armed criminal, I am quite willing to destroy him if I need to. If it turns out that the person I encounter is innocent, I would simply lower the gun muzzle upon recognition and not shoot. Problems here can be prevented by observing rule three.

Rule Three: *Keep your finger off the trigger until your sights are on the target.* Remember that in the tactical scenario, your sights are not on the target yet. This is a last fail-safe device that prevents unintentional shots. When moving tactically "on the hunt," the trigger finger is straight alongside the pistol frame. When drawing or otherwise handling the pistol in administrative or tactical situations, keep the finger off the trigger.

Rule Four: *Be sure of your target and what is beyond it.* Do not shoot at a sound or a shadow; it might not be what you think. There is no greater tragedy than to realize that you've just shot a loved one by mistake. Almost as bad is to shoot an innocent stranger. Don't let this happen to you—be sure of your target.

Also be aware of what is beyond the object of your shooting. Sometimes the hazard of overpenetration will arise. This means bullets that exit the adversary on the side opposite from where you've shot him might pose a threat to uninvolved parties behind him. There are methods to minimize the possibility of hitting innocents in such situations—learn them!

None of these rules are based on mechanical safety devices but rather on mind-set. They are applicable for life, and you must always observe them when handling firearms.

FIREARMS TRAINING INSTITUTE

1. *Every* gun is *always* loaded.

2. *Never* let the muzzle cover anything you are not willing to destroy.

3. Keep your finger *OFF* the trigger until your sights are *on the target!*

4. *Always* be sure of your target.

The four essential rules of firearms safety as developed by Jeff Cooper and taught at the Front Sight Firearms Training Institute.

The Dynamics of a Gunfight

Several centuries ago, the medieval general Sun Tzu wrote that, next to knowing his own capabilities, a successful warrior must also know his probable opponent's disposition as well as the nature of the likely battlefield. You can approach the study of gunfighting in the same manner. No two shootings are identical, but you can study the statistical trends of gunfights and note recurring patterns and similarities. You can examine how people react under fire. You can gather intelligence the way a general gathers intelligence about his enemy. Then you can arrange your training priorities accordingly to reflect the reality of what you will likely be up against. You want to "play the averages" in your preparation but still consider the worst-case scenario that you can realistically expect.

During practice, keep true to the spirit of the exercise and train with the gear you are likely to have on hand when the shooting starts. Remember the old adage, "You will fight like you've trained, so train like you intend to fight!"

In general, gunfights tend to be exhilarating affairs. Regardless of your level of readiness, your systems will probably be supercharged with high-octane racing adrenaline. Generally, the more warning of trouble that you have, the more gradual the effects of the adrenaline will be. Everyone will experience to some degree a state of extreme alarm and the subsequent effects of the startle reflex on their bodies.

The physical manifestations of the startle reflex are important to consider, because you must organize your training with them in mind. Remember: expect the worst, train for it, and hope for the best.

The physical reactions you experience to a sudden threat are, to a certain degree, automatic, and have been termed the fight/flight response. The fight/flight response is a chemical reaction within the body to the startle reflex. It is characterized by diminished motor skills, confusion, narrowing of visual and auditory focus, and rapid heartbeat. This response is within us from the days when men fought with clubs, lived in caves, and ate raw meat. It is easy for us to characterize these physical responses as "being scared."

The word "scared," however, seems to be associated instantly with the word "fear." It is not the same as fear. Fear requires mental analysis of the situation, and that takes time to do. In a gunfight, you generally will not have that luxury. Additionally, scary fear is exactly the opposite of what you need to feel in order to place your shots accurately. A better characterization of these physical responses is "a state of extreme alarm."

When you find yourself in a state of extreme alarm, there will be a tendency to lose fine motor skills. Finger dexterity will be adversely affected, creating a state of "fumble fingers." This means that you need to make all of your gun-handling actions large, positive, and simple movements. Avoid unnecessary complexity in all your training. Where does this leave the man who must unlatch several safety devices before he can get his gun working? Or the man who must disengage a minuscule safety latch on his sidearm before firing? Training will help with such activities, but only to a point. The fight/flight reflex will short circuit your training if you do not train with those effects in mind. The rule of thumb: *keep things simple!*

You may experience difficulty in making critical decisions and an inability to keep track of your thoughts as your mind goes into hyperspeed. Normal intellectual analysis will be hampered to some degree, and you will fall back on your conditioned responses. The ultimate goal of any training program should be to ingrain those conditioned responses into the mind's neural pathways—there's no time for mental discussions in a gunfight. You must excise as many potential decisions from your act of shooting as possible. Doing this will prevent indecision about "how" to execute that act as your system goes on auto pilot. This frees the mind to consider when to shoot rather than how to do so.

Rapidly unfolding events will tend to get jumbled in the memory banks as the mind tries to process information at ultrahigh speed. Anything in the combat response that demands keeping a mental track of something should be looked at with suspicion. It will, for example, be difficult to maintain a running tally of rounds fired. If your indication to reload is having reached a certain count, you will likely end up with an empty gun. You need to seek other stimuli to tell you there is a need to reload.

Your attention will initially be drawn directly to the source of the danger. There will be a tendency to exclude everything else, and secondary lateral targets may be overlooked. Some police trainers have called this "tunnel vision." Mentally you may dismiss what you think is nonessential information, and you may not even remember specifics about it later. It is important to scan for secondary targets immediately after the original threat has been neutralized. You can do this by training yourself to look right and left after each firing string prior to reholstering. Move the gun muzzle along with the eyes to be able to react instantly if a second or third target is located.

Your listening will also be affected. You might ignore peripheral sounds, thinking them to be unimportant. During one incident, I distinctly remember thinking that the sound of my shotgun did not seem nearly as loud or as sharp as on the firing range. Other seemingly inconsequential sounds like a pistol slide going into battery or the front door of a liquor store opening will be amplified and quite distinct. Hearing a threat can be just as valuable a target indicator as seeing a threat, so do not dismiss either one. Laterally scanning after engagement helps diffuse the intense attention focused on one particular threat. It also reminds you to *listen* laterally as well.

Your body, of course, will tend to tense up. Alarm reactions will include rapid heartbeat, rapid breathing, and a general state of excitement. When these are coupled with an attack of fumble fingers, it will be difficult to conduct any complicated motor skill. This is why you must develop large, simple, basic gun-handling movements. This is also the reason to keep fingers *off* triggers until you are on target.

You may experience distortion of time and distance. Remember that your mind will be operating at hyperspeed. For some, this will seem to make time move in slow motion. This same mental acceleration will tend to make distant things seem closer.

Not everyone will experience these effects. They seem to be tied to the amount of surprise one experiences. Those who are taken completely unaware will probably experience all of them. On the other hand, a man who knows he will be in a fight has the advantage and will generally not experience them as intensely. Although you should constantly try to maintain an alert mind-set, you cannot predict your level of readiness and expectation. Keep these things in mind when conducting training and practice sessions. You must seek to minimize your vulnerability to these alarm effects by keeping things simple, maintaining uniformity in your gun-handling practice, and establishing conditioned responses that you can rely on. Train like you intend to fight!

I'll let you in on a couple of secrets. First, the better physical condition you are in, the less you will fall victim to these effects. The reason is that a well-conditioned body can operate at a higher level than a poorly conditioned one and is better prepared to handle the sudden adrenaline in the system. This means that you must drop the post-range Hostess Twinkies and attempt to establish a modicum of physical fitness. You do not need to become Olympians, just physically fit.

Second, subsequent life-death encounters will probably not cause the same extreme alarm sensations. As unpopular a view as this is, it does get easier to handle the second and even third time around. Rather than extreme alarm, you might feel the same excitement you would if you were a soccer goalie during the last play of a tied game.

Police gunfight scenarios will differ slightly from those of private citizens. The reason is that police officers must often seek and close in on armed criminals, in essence taking the fight to them. Private citizens, on the other hand, always avoid criminals if they can. If that is not possible, then their circumstances will likely be of an even more reactive nature than police encounters. Police officers might have other assisting officers present, whereas private citizens will likely be alone. The battlefields and tactics will tend to differ slightly, but the nature of the fight will remain the same.

Studying a synopsis of police shootings for the past year shows that distances involved tend to be very close. More than 80 percent of gunfights occurred within the typical 7 yard distance. Over half of those happened within the back-slapping range of 5 feet or less! What does this tell you about tactics? You must maximize your distance from the threat and minimize your exposure to it. The greater the distance, the more the advantage goes to the trained shooter. Any nimrod can get lucky within 5 feet, and luck is one of the uncontrollable factors in a fight. What does this tell you about your training? Most of it should be within 7 yards. If you think that more than 80 percent of it should be within that distance, you are starting to get the picture.

Even though you may not need to shoot a man farther away than 20 feet, it is important to be able to reach out and hit someone across the street too, because 15 percent of fights occur at distances exceeding 50 feet. So take 15 percent of your drills out to 25 yards, 50 yards, and farther. Every so often, it is important to try a few shots at 100 yards to see what the bullet drop is for the weapon system. The chances of having to deck someone a football field away are slim, but then again . . .

Gunfights tend to be sudden and violent. The estimated elapsed time is roughly 3 seconds. A large majority of shootings involve moving suspects. The message is clear. Shoot as fast as you can hit! Don't seek to hit the adversary's breast pocket button in 3 seconds. Rather, a single hit somewhere on the chest in 1.5 seconds is more realistic. You must balance speed and accuracy within the context of the problem.

About 70 percent of gunfights occur in reduced light environments. Criminals, like roaches, fear the light. Do not conduct all of your training outdoors at high noon. Try to secure an opportunity to shoot in reduced light at least occasionally. Doing so will point out the problems and solutions for low-light environments. Private citizens might not go around with a Mag-Light in their belt to complement a pistol, but police officers do. There are ways to coordinate light and gun—learn them!

Almost 50 percent of the time you might face more than one assailant. Any brief study of the habits of armed robbers shows that they rarely act alone, so practice multiple-target drills. The rule of thumb is to hit each hostile once until he is down or running away. Repeat as necessary (more on this later). Refrain from placing all your practice targets in a neat row like good Napoleonic soldiers at inspection time. Stagger the distances. Place some high and others low, in divergent angles, and behind cover. Make it difficult for yourself—the bad guys will! Push yourself faster and faster until you find the limit of your skill. Then seek to extend that limit! As the wise man said, "The more we sweat in training, the less we bleed in combat." Amen!

Sharpening the Mental Trigger

Combat mind-set and tactical shooting are irrevocably intertwined. We studied the various conditions of readiness in Chapter 2. When you have a specific alert—i.e., a possible target—you are in fact waiting for a cue from that possible target to shoot. That cue will be some unmistakable action or series of actions that will indicate that an attack is in progress. You set the mental trigger when you go on specific alert (condition orange). The cue from the target that signals the attack will release the mental trigger and propel you into condition red (fight in progress), bringing forth the killing response.

The mechanics of using the pistol for defensive purposes involve not only the physical act of drawing and firing but also the visual acquisition of the target and the mental analysis that determines if it is a threat. This visual acquisition and mental analysis precede shooting and determine how fast you respond in a real-world situation.

Target acquisition is a product of your own awareness and the perceived actions of your would-be antagonist. Determination of threat depends on what that individual is holding in his hands. You must look and see what your adversary is doing with or holding in his hands.

Train so that the cue that triggers the killing response is not the audible tone from your shooting timers nor the shrill whine of a rangemaster's whistle but rather is provided by the target/threat himself. Think about it. If you encounter a possible threat, a threat that you may have to terminate quickly by gunfire, the signal to do so will be an action by the threat itself. It will not be a signal from an uninvolved third party.

The people I work for purchased an interactive computer/video training system recently that is the state of the art (this week, anyway). The system presents a big-screen video scenario involving deadly force situations likely to be encountered by an officer. The officer, armed with a laser-equipped pistol, interacts with the images on the screen, sometimes "shooting" them. The interfaced computer tallies any shots fired as well as reaction times and other pertinent factors. The system is complete with foul-mouthed criminals and sound-effect gunfire.

The most valuable thing about the system is that it makes the shooter look to the actual target and analyze it quickly for a cue or a reason to shoot, just like in real life! It is a good training tool indeed but, at the same price as a modest house in the country, only a viable option if the taxpayers sign the check.

Do not despair. With a little ingenuity and a clear understanding of what you are trying to accomplish, you can develop exercises to obtain the attributes you seek. What you are after is the habit of looking at the target for visual determination of threat status. You need to look at the target, analyze what you see, and act on your determination of threat level. Only after you've done this mentally will it even occur to you that shooting is required, but that realization is what the mental trigger is all about. As you can see, the time spent on acquisition and analysis greatly affects your response time.

This response time can be shortened by the following exercise. Begin by painting four different shapes on an IPSC (International Practical Shooting Confederation) humanoid target. The shapes are not a serious issue but should be substantially different from one another to be able to distinguish them at a glance. The shapes I use are a square, circle, triangle, and diamond. A stencil can be made from a piece of cardboard to facilitate spraypainting these onto the target. I've found that it works best to use drab, neutral colors for the shapes, such as olive green, black, gray, and brown. These colors do not stand out, and the shooter must work harder to distinguish them. Training is supposed to be difficult, right?

With four shapes and four colors, you have a possible 16 different combinations of shapes and colors. One target can hold six different shapes. One shape/color combination should not be repeated on any single target.

Take four such targets to the shooting range and set them up at the typical distance where most shoot-outs occur of 5 to 7 yards. Face 180 degrees away from the target array and stand by. A training partner will call out a color/shape combination and immediately signal to shoot. At his signal, turn to face the targets, scan them, locate the shape/color in question, and shoot that shape in its center!

If a training partner is not available, it is a simple matter to get 16 business cards and draw a facsimile of one color/shape combination on each card. Place the cards in a coffee can at your feet as you face away from the target array. Retrieve a card without looking at it (be honest) and hold onto it until the shooting timer (which you've programmed for delayed start) gives the audible beep. Look at the card and see what shape and color is represented, let the card fall to the deck, and turn to face the targets. Scan the targets, locate the required shape/color, and shoot it as soon as you find it! As this becomes easy to do, you can select two cards and repeat the drill with two target indicators. Note that some targets may not have any of the shapes/colors selected. These targets represent uninvolved innocents in the scenario and cannot be even nicked by a bullet.

The next evolution of this drill is to substitute the painted shapes and colors with the popular Duel-a-tron type targets. The latest generation of these targets can be equipped with paste-on accessories to change their threat level. These accessories range from a camera to a broken bottle and from a pistol to a policeman's undercover badge and can be placed "in" the target's hands to dictate when a terminal response is required.

The drill does not change except that it requires a partner to equip the targets as you are facing away from them. Oh yes, one more thing—the targets are now staggered close and far rather than all lined up ready for inspection!

At the signal, turn and scan the targets just as you did with the shape/color portion. This time, however, you must scan *the hands*. Determine hostile targets by looking and seeing what they have in their hands, just like in real life. A target with a weapon is a hostile target and must be shot forthwith. You do not negotiate with an armed man!

Be careful not to direct your shots at what the target is holding, as many unknowingly do. You must notice the weapon in the target's hand and respond to that target with gunfire, placing the shots in the vitals.

Not only must you locate and determine threat level, but you also have to prioritize the targets and shoot the ones most immediately capable of killing you. For example, a man with a knife at arm's length is more dangerous than a man with a pistol at 7 yards. To complicate things, you can do the drill on the move, in the dark, and with various weapons.

You cannot get complacent and think you are ready for combat because you can react to the start tone generated by the shooting timer. You need to look at the targets—they will tell you when to shoot and when not to. And it is the hands and what they carry that will kill, so it is the hands and what they carry that decides the adversary's fate.

The Presentation

The pistol is, conceptually, a reactive device. It is worn constantly on the person in general anticipation of an unexpected fight. Clearly, if you received notice of an impending assault, you would obtain a more powerful weapon such as a rifle or shotgun, but more likely than not, the weapon you have with you when trouble starts will be the pistol. In those cases when it is really needed, it will be needed in an eye blink.

The act of making the pistol instantly available from a condition of unreadiness is an important skill to master. This presentation or "draw" can be accomplished from a desk drawer, a driver's console in an automobile, or a lady's purse. But by far the predominant method of carry is the strong-side hip holster.

A study of proper holsters could easily encompass an entire volume, and that is clearly not the purpose here. Suffice to say that a proper holster allows the wearer to bring his pistol into action with a minimum of effort and fanfare. A proper holster will also hold the pistol tight enough to retain it during reasonably violent physical activity. The two factors must be equally balanced. Whatever type is chosen, it is important to wear the holster in the same position at all

The presentation begins from a relaxed posture.

The first step is the GRIP.

Step two, CLEAR, gets the pistol out and to a position alongside the strong-side pectoral muscle.

Step three brings the strong hand and support hand together in front of the chest in a sort of clapping action.

Step four has the shooter extending the pistol toward the target, taking up the slack, and thinking *FRONT SIGHT!*

After the necessary shots have been fired, or if no shots are required, the pistol is lowered only enough to be able to see the adversary's hands.

This ready position is too low.

times. A lightning-quick presentation requires the development of reflexive actions. A man would be severely embarrassed (maybe to death) to reach for his strong-side hip holster only to remember on arrival that he was wearing a shoulder rig! Sometimes you must vary your carry method, but you should try to minimize those times as much as you can.

A well-executed presentation brings the pistol from holster to target in the most efficient and direct manner possible while observing realistic safety precautions. A student first learning to draw his pistol will execute the particular moves step by step in sharp staccato fashion, taking care that the muzzle does not cover anything on the way to the target and that the trigger finger is kept clear of the trigger.

The following steps are described for a strong-side hip holster but can be easily modified to suit any particular carry style.

The first step moves the strong hand onto the pistol. It must grip the pistol as high on the grip frame as possible. The hand grips the pistol with the last three fingers. The trigger finger remains straight alongside the holster and the thumb is "flagged" like a hitchhiker's along the rear of the pistol's slide. This grip will keep the fingers from snagging on any clothing. If the holster includes any retention snap, it is disengaged at this point.

The grip must be the same every time. The initial grip is what actually indexes the pistol and allows it to point at what the eyes are looking at. This grip must be learned by feel so that the hand "knows" where the pistol must be gripped.

Simultaneously, the support hand moves to a position in front of the left pectoral muscle. It is held vertically with the fingers cupped, ready to intercept the forthcoming pistol. If a concealment garment is worn to hide the pistol, the strong-side hand begins positioned at the sternum and sweeps the covering garment aside as it moves toward the pistol. This first "step" is the most important and must be practiced until it becomes a reflex!

From the grip position the pistol is brought out of the holster and up to a point just under the strong-side pectoral muscle, with the muzzle parallel to the deck and pointed toward the target. The trigger finger remains extended alongside the pistol and *off* the trigger. The strong-hand thumb takes a position on the side of the pistol. In fact, at the beginning level you can use the strong-hand thumb touching the right pec as an index point in the draw. The support hand remains positioned under the left pectoral muscle and the eyes are looking at the target.

At the third step, the strong-side hand brings the pistol to the support hand, which joins with it in a two-handed grip in a sort of clapping fashion. If the pistol is equipped with a safety, it is disengaged now. The pistol is still parallel with the deck and leveled at the target. The eyes are still "downrange" looking at the source of the threat. The pistol's muzzle does not cover the support hand at any time during this maneuver. The trigger finger enters the trigger guard at this point but does not contact the trigger if the pistol is a single-action type. If it is a double-action, the trigger finger touches the trigger but does not begin to press. It is important to realize that if the threat closes the gap, the pistol can be fired easily at this or the previous position.

The support hand grips over the strong-hand fingers. The strong-hand thumb extends forward along the frame and points at the target. The support thumb also points forward along the frame just under the strong-hand thumb. The support thumb actually creates a shelf for the strong-hand thumb to press down on. There is pressure exerted fore and aft by the strong hand pushing into the support hand. There is also side to side pressure created by the palms of the hands

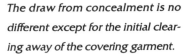

The draw from concealment is no different except for the initial clearing away of the covering garment.

The strong hand begins high up on the vest . . .

pressing against each other and by the support fingers actually squeezing the entire package. This grip allows the pistol to return consistently on recoil. The consistency of return determines how fast you will be able to fire a second shot.

The final position involves simply extending the strong-side arm toward the target and moving the support elbow down to point at the deck in a perfect Weaver shooting platform. The eyes are initially looking at the threat, but as the pistol enters the line of sight, the visual focus is shifted to the sights (the front sight in particular). If the pistol is a single-action type, the trigger finger executes the final press and fires the shot. With a double-action, the trigger

. . . and sweeps down and back as   *GRIP!*
it moves toward the pistol.

press is begun as the strong-side arm begins to extend. The hammer reaches the zenith of its arc as the pistol aligns on target. When the eye verifies the alignment, the shot is fired.

If the decision to shoot is made prior to the presentation, the pistol is brought directly to the target and the shot is fired. If there is no immediate need to shoot, the pistol is brought to the guard position. The guard position has been taught in the past at its extreme lowest point, with the pistol pointing at the deck. This is useful to demonstrate the difference between being on target and being on guard, but it is not an efficient way to settle social disputes. If

Continue as before until the pistol is on target.

shooting your adversary is not the initial plan, then the draw proceeds to the guard position low enough to enable you to still see the adversary's hands but not lower. This usually means holding the muzzle at approximately the belt line of the adversary. The pistol is still pointing at the adversary, since you are quite willing to kill him if you need to, but your eyes have not shifted to the sights and your trigger finger has not acquired the trigger. The visual focus is on the target itself, but the sights are visible in the peripheral field.

Natural progression involves smoothing the rough edges as superfluous motion is deleted. There is a natural tendency to attempt speed. This must be resisted. Rather than trying to "go fast," try to decrease the time it takes to get the pistol aligned on target. Try to eliminate any wasted motion and actually do less to accomplish the same goal. If you are smooth, you will be fast.

The ultimate level is to develop a reflexive presentation. The way to achieve that objective is through thousands of repetitions, fully concentrating on the act itself. This will program the movement into the neural pathways and develop muscle memory. The result will be unconscious reflexive execution, where conscious thought about "how" to execute the action will not be necessary. Instead, you simply decide to act—the programmed reflexes do the rest.

This level of skill does not come easily or cheaply. The price is endless repetition and the currency is dry firing. Combat shooting involves the ability to execute preestablished physiomotor skills under stressful situations. The more you are physically accustomed to executing those skills, the less concentration you will need to devote to them in times of crisis because they will become automatic. The best known method for accomplishing this is by handling and dry firing an unloaded pistol regularly and repetitively.

To avoid having to explain embarrassing bullet holes in the living room wall, make sure that the pistol is indeed unloaded. It is also advisable to secure any live ammunition in a room away from the training area. If you are called away for any reason, when you return it is important to recheck the status of the pistol to reinsure it is unloaded.

To inject some realism to the drill, it is a good idea to use a humanoid cardboard cutout target. In addition, placing the target about 5 to 7 yards away will teach you about real distance as well as real time. Begin slowly—again, the goal is smoothness, not speed. Proceed through the entire drawing sequence from the grip through the hammer fall. Include the all-important shift of visual focus from target to sights, and take particular care to keep the trigger finger clear of the trigger until the right time. Focus all the concentration on executing the draw. Do not let the mind wander—pay attention to the draw as it is happening. What you practice is what you will execute in a fight. As the computer people say, "garbage in/garbage out."

At advanced levels, the use of a shooting timer is essential for dry firing. Set the par-time feature for the specific time interval for one repetition. Such a timer will give audible signals at the beginning and end of the interval. The object is to execute the draw within that interval.

Learn the basics step by step. Then refine those basics with directness and economy of motion. Then establish the result as conditioned reflexes with proper continuous practice. The result will be that someone trying to kill you by surprise will be in more danger from you than you are from him!

The Flash Sight Picture

(Previously published in *Soldier of Fortune* magazine, November 1994, under the title "Get the Picture.")

It is important to realize that while you do not use the sights to align the pistol in the sense of a bull's-eye shooter aligning his sights on target, you do use the sights for almost all combat shooting. The exception is closest-quarters, weapon-retention, belly-button range where you can actually touch your adversary with the gun muzzle.

There is a great difference, however, in how much time you *spend* looking at the sights. This difference corresponds with the difficulty of the shot that you are about to make. In order to be successful, you need to know how sharp of a focus on the sights that shot requires. That requirement will be different for a 5 yard as-fast-as-you-can-hammer aimed at the adversary's chest than for a hostage situation head shot at the same distance. The requirements will be different again for a chest shot at 50 yards. You need to learn what quality of sight picture you need to see in order to make the shot.

In all circumstances, you must do several things in succession. First identify the target. But not only must you I.D. the target, you must identify the exact spot on that target that you wish to hit. Your visual focus must be on that exact spot so that your muscles will know where to move the pistol when you think "GO." Initially, look at the target's hands to determine if he is, in fact, a threat. What those hands contain (gun, knife, camera, badge, etc.) will determine your response. But as soon as a threat is realized, shift your visual focus to the target spot.

Think of it as looking at the target with a telephoto lens instead of a wide-angle lens. So instead of looking at the adversary's head, look at the spot between his eyes. Instead of looking at the adversary's chest, look at the shirt button in the middle of his chest.

Do not confuse this with tunnel vision. It is not. With tunnel vision, peripheral vision is discounted. With target focus, you consciously see the spot you want to hit but are also aware of what you see in your peripheral field of vision. Just like gun-handling skills and mind-set, the way you "look" at targets (and what is around them) needs to be practiced.

The presentation of the pistol itself must be smooth, refined, and shorn of all superfluous movements. This is where all those thousands of repetitions we discussed in the previous chapter come in. Rather than thinking about the movements of the draw, you will simply think "GO!" Where you will "go" is wherever your eyes are looking, and that is why you need to focus on the spot you want to hit instead of just seeing the entire target. Where your eyes go your attention follows, and where your attention goes the pistol follows.

Try this experiment to illustrate the point. Look at a target's chest and then, without shifting the visual focus, bring the pistol to bear on the target's head. To illustrate further, look at one target, then draw and bring the pistol to bear on a separate target. It isn't easy, is it. It actually feels quite unnatural. Now look again at the original target. Look at the very spot you would like to hit and then draw to that spot. See how easy it is!

Once the pistol reaches the target spot, it must stop on that spot long enough to shoot it. You must see it stop in order to be certain that the shot will go where it was intended to go. The progression is seeing the spot you wish to hit, moving the pistol to that spot, and stopping the pistol on that spot.

As the pistol stops on target, shift your visual focus from the target spot to the front sight. You are still aware of the target in relation to your position and your sights, but you are not actively "looking" for it. As you see the front sight aligned on that target spot, you break the shot.

Ideally, the pistol stopping on the target spot, the shift of visual focus, and the breaking of the shot will occur simultaneously. In very close-range scenarios, this is usually the case because you are moving as fast as humanly possible—all you do is keep up visually with the physical activity. Not only are you moving quickly, you are also "looking" quickly.

When ranges increase or the difficulty of the shot intensifies, you will find yourself spending more time on the sights to make *extra* sure you are "on." With practice you will know what quality of sight picture you need to see for each particular shot. Just because you can get away with relatively coarse sight pictures up close does not mean that you can get away with not seeing any sight picture at all.

It is equally important to see the front sight just as the shot breaks and to see that front sight leave the target spot on recoil. The point on the target where you see the front sight leave the target will generally be where the shot will go. If you haven't noticed what the front sight does in recoil before, look for it from now on. It will make a big difference.

In the dark, our system doesn't change. Without getting into a discussion of sight enhancements and flashlight techniques, the kinesthetic alignment you develop will enable you to get the pistol on target in the dark as easily as you do at high noon. The only problems are locating and identifying the target, which will need to be done regardless of your shooting style.

Shifting your visual focus to the sights to verify your kinesthetic index of the pistol on target takes no more time than simply hauling the pistol out and breaking a shot with your eyes closed. But it will let you hit what you want to hit. The most important thing is that you must strive to make all of this automatic through continuous and attentive practice.

Using the sights properly within the requirements of the tactical situation is just as fast as any so-called instinctive method. More importantly, it allows you to hit, and that is what the combat use of the pistol is all about. You want to get solid hits in the least time possible on another man who is bent on killing you! In training, you must condition your mind that you are "playing for keeps." When you feel the temptation to ignore the sight picture, remind yourself that *if you miss, you die.* Do you feel lucky?

Firing Modes with the Combat Pistol

(Previously published in *Soldier of Fortune* magazine, January 1995, under the title "Two Hits per Customer.")

The Modern Technique of the Pistol promotes the "standard defensive response" to an attack—two quick shots to the chest. The reasons for two shots instead of one are because even the most powerful pistols cannot be counted on for 100 percent stopping power, and two shots tend to multiply that power. This reaches a point of diminishing returns after two shots because the adversary's nervous system generally becomes desensitized to further shots. Additionally, two shots increase your chance of obtaining at least one solid hit on difficult targets since there is always the possibility that you might miss with the first shot (horrors!).

The method you use to deliver those two quick shots varies with the tactical situation. The cadence depends on the target's proximity. Generally, the closer the adversary, the faster you can shoot and still hit (depending on individual ability, of course). Conversely, the farther a target is, the longer you may take to shoot. This makes perfect sense when you realize that a closer target is both a much easier target and a much greater threat than a distant target. Time to react increases with distance. This way a target at 5 feet must be hit much faster than a target at 50 yards.

The first firing mode and the most basic is the "controlled pair." Think of the controlled pair as two one-shot strings. You shoot and hit with the first shot and only fire the second shot when you have reacquired the sight picture and made any necessary adjustments to realign the pistol.

Continuous practice decreases the time interval between shots due to enhanced recoil control and the development of a solid, proper firing platform. Such a firing platform (Weaver stance) allows the pistol to return back from recoil to the same general alignment as the first shot. The speed with which the pistol returns to the target determines the speed with which you will be able to fire the second shot.

The second firing mode is a natural progression from the first one, differing only in the accelerated cadence. This mode is called the "dedicated pair."

The closer you find yourself to your adversary, the faster you must hit him. For closest encounters within the magical 7-yard range, we use "the hammer." This term, coined at the old American Pistol Institute, indicates a cadence substantially accelerated from the previous two shooting methods. Think of the hammer not as two one-shot strings but as one two-shot string.

In a hammer, you use the flash sight picture for the first shot as fast as you can hit. As soon as you recover from the arc of recoil and the pistol indexes back on target, you shoot again. You may try to pick up a glance at the sight picture, but do not "wait" to see it. Simply time the second shot to coincide with the return of the axis of the bore to the target. Again, you will find that a proper firing platform provided by the Weaver stance allows the pistol to return back into place through muscle memory and because of its muzzle-flip dampening qualities.

Think of the controlled pair as "sight/shoot/recover/verify/alignment/sight/shoot." The dedicated pair is "sight/shoot/recover/sight/shoot." The only real difference between the two is the accelerated cadence. The hammer is "sight/shoot/hang on/shoot."

Another variation developed by Colonel Cooper is called the "split hammer." This is a very specialized technique for sorting out two adversaries who are standing close together. You hit the first man with the first shot of the two-shot string. Then you shift the pistol laterally on recoil, using the time between shots to "travel" to the second man. When you arrive at the second man you shoot. You may see the front sight superimposed on the second target's chest, but you will not "wait" to see it. Using this technique on two targets at a distance of 5 yards, you can expect times less than 1.5 seconds for two solid hits.

There are other firing modes that seem to be natural progressions of the previous drills. One of them is the Mozambique drill. The Mozambique involves following up the two shots (of any cadence) with a carefully placed brain shot. The theory behind the Mozambique drill is that the two shots didn't have the desired effect. This occurs quite often in our age of body armor, small calibers, and widespread drug use. Rather than pummel the adversary's desensitized or possibly armored body with bullets until you run out, you shift to Plan B, place a single shot in the data base, and turn off the machine.

The classic Mozambique drill calls for a pause and evaluation after the first two shots to see if they've worked. If they have not, you proceed with the head shot. This will be discussed more in Chapter 10 dealing with stopping power.

This technique calls for a distinct shift in gears as you shoot. The first two shots are going to be very quick. If you proceed from the evaluation phase to the head shot, the impulse is to shoot it as fast as the first two shots were fired. This will probably produce a fast miss. You have to slow down consciously and get that hit. I suggest timing the first two shots and not timing the head shot in training situations. This in effect creates an open-end time interval to make the hit and establish correct habits. (Don't confuse the open-end interval with unlimited time because you still have a requirement to hit as soon as you can.) If you miss, you die! Allowing enough time within reason to make the shot encourages the marksman's pause that you need here.

The Mozambique drill dates back to the hostilities several years ago in (you guessed it) Mozambique, Africa. A man named John Rouseau was on his way to the airport to catch the "last flight out" when he rounded a corner and was confronted by an individual charging at him with an AK-47. Suitably alarmed, Rouseau hammered him in the chest with his Browning Hi-Power. Convinced that the issue had been settled, he brought his pistol down to the ready position in order to admire his handiwork and was astounded to see his antagonist still charging.

Rouseau reportedly brought his pistol up in a hurry with the intent of shooting for the brain but hit him between the clavicles and broke the spine instead. This was obviously not the actual plan, but it worked.

Controlled pair, dedicated pair, or hammer always mean two hits per customer. How those hits are delivered and what happens afterward need to be thought about and practiced before the fight occurs. Those who are destined to win study first, then fight. Those destined to lose fight first and then (if they're still alive) study why they've lost.

Training the Startle Response

(Previously published in *Soldier of Fortune* magazine, July 1994, under the title "Reaction Reflex.")

I was once told that a general might be forgiven for losing a battle but never for being surprised by the enemy. Modern thinking in the field of weaponcraft also presumes that being surprised by an aggressor is tantamount to defeat. We are taught that with a properly organized "combat mind-set," the possibility of being taken unaware and surprised by a foe is almost nil. This is as it should be because anytime we wear pistols (and otherwise), we must be extra attentive to our surroundings. This, in turn, tends to keep us free from surprise.

As much as we hate to admit it, we are human and fallible, and our attentive combat mind-set sometimes falters. When this happens, we lapse into that dreaded state of unreadiness called condition white.

If you are attacked while inattentive to your surroundings, your trained response will be delayed substantially while you try to play mental catch-up. Instead of a proper combat response, you will experience a big flinch, characterized by tensing the muscles, hunching the shoulders, bending the knees, bringing the hands up to protect the face, and, worst of all, closing the eyes. This is called the startle reflex. It is

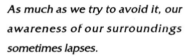

As much as we try to avoid it, our awareness of our surroundings sometimes lapses.

Training and developing a strong reflex to a danger stimulus will keep us ready and . . .

simply a reflexive "jump" to a sudden fright stimulus, and it is no way to win a fight.

To be fully prepared for life's unexpected social disagreements, you need to examine your fighting response from conditions of total unreadiness. Your trained response will be delayed if you are surprised. The startle reflex, on the other hand, is not delayed but rather is instantaneous. Experience has shown that with proper training, you can convert the frightful flinch into a fighting move! That fighting move, of course, is the first step of the pistol draw—the grip.

There has been some discussion that if you are going to make the grip into a startle reflex, why not make the whole presentation a startle reflex? I don't recommend it.

. . . on target, even if startled.

Remember that we are not discussing a circumstance where you know that a particular antagonist is trying to harm you and you see him commit himself enough to shoot him. We are looking at a situation where you were not paying attention. Since you were not paying attention, you don't have a particular target or even a confirmed threat. You don't necessarily want to draw and shoot without knowing what is going on, but you do want to go for the grip instead of flinching uncontrollably away from a fright stimulus. Drawing and shooting at everything that startles you is not advisable in most circumstances. A simple grip allows you to assess the situation and establish if there is a need to act further. If there is, then you are in the best position to do so with a hand on the holstered pistol.

There are three steps to developing a reflexive tactical response from a startle reflex. The first step is to have practiced the full proper draw several thousand times. This extensive repetition will overdevelop and enhance the neural pathways that take the message from the brain to the hand that says, "DRAW." This allows the body to memorize the movements and execute them on demand without any analytical thinking. Do not attempt to force speed in the draw; rather, develop smoothness and correct moves.

Visualization or mental rehearsal is the next step. This

mental imagery will enhance the reflexes that all the previous repetitions will have developed. You must convince yourself mentally that you will respond as you've been trained to respond when you're startled. In this creative daydream, imagine yourself in a quiet, calm situation. Then visualize being startled suddenly. In the mental drill, your response to the sudden fright stimulus must be what you've programmed yourself to respond with. The grip is your initial response, and the remainder of the presentation will be a follow-through to deal with the threat.

Step three is to practice the same drill physically in real-time. Make the pistol ready for dry firing, observing all the usual precautions associated with that practice. Holster the pistol and select a sound that will serve as a startle stimulus (the tape-recorded sound of gunshots, for example). Now simply rig the tape recorder to a timer such as the kind used to turn lights on and off in the home while you are on vacation. Ideally, you should include some sort of visual cue from the target, but until technology catches up to training need, the audible cue will have to do. Next, set the timer delay for two or three minutes and just relax. Initially it is best to perform this drill in a standing posture, but as you progress you may add sitting, reclining, and other positions of unreadiness.

Now try to forget about the forthcoming sound and simply relax and be "unready." When the sound "startles" you, force yourself to go to the grip step of the draw in a strong, positive manner. At first you will notice that there is greater lag-time than when you are "ready." Not to worry—the more you practice, the less lag-time you will exhibit. The key to this drill is to let the sound you've recorded actually startle you in order to program the proper response under the right conditions. It is helpful to vary the recording to avoid becoming accustomed to one sound. After you've performed this drill the desired number of times, perform several full and complete draws to re-establish the entire combat response in your mind.

Since the object of the drill is to react to a surprise, realize that your hands will probably be occupied when you see the need to shoot. Therefore, it is paramount to train yourself to drop whatever you are holding when you need to react to the threat. It may vary from a cup of coffee to a cigar to the week's groceries. You don't need to waste good coffee or even good cigars, however. Simple cardboard boxes of varying sizes and Styrofoam cups can substitute for the real thing in practice. When the whistle blows, simply discard the article by letting it fall as you move for the pistol. Do not waste time by casting the item aside; instead, simply open the hands and move for the pistol with no concern for whatever it is that you've dropped.

Converting the startle response into a tactical response also tends to forestall fright and panic. The grip of the draw is a very forceful and positive action that tends to remind us of the skills that we've learned and sends our minds in the "right direction" during unscheduled social disagreements. What follows is usually the intense concentration on sight picture and trigger press that has saved lives. Moving to grip is an aggressive fight response that will overshadow the startle reflex. This aggressive posture will set the tone for the rest of the fight.

There is no question that the best defense is to realize that there is going to be a fight before it starts and take steps to win it without being surprised. There is also no question that you need to practice for the worst case. But you must also examine and develop your defensive reflexes on occasions when you might lapse into unreadiness. The drills outlined here will do just that. If you develop a tactical response from your startle reflex, you will never be surprised—even when you are!

chapter 10

Stopping Power and Shot Placement

One of the most prevalent discussions in the field of tactical shooting is that of stopping power. That quaint phrase refers, of course, to the ability (or lack thereof) of a particular cartridge to incapacitate a human adversary. Reams of material have been written on the subject by those who should know about these things and even more by those who do not know anything but think they do.

There are generally two schools of thought on the issue. One group favors the light, high-speed, small-caliber hollow-point bullet of .38/.357/9mm persuasion. Advocates of this concept rely on the theoretical expansion of these high-speed wonder bullets in the body of the shootee to create massive physical damage and thereby incapacitation. They point to their chosen bullet's performance in ballistic gelatin and claim the same performance in human flesh.

The other group advocates the use of large-caliber bullets of comparatively slower velocity. They believe that expansion is not required if you begin with a large bullet in the first place. They place their faith in the fact that a large bullet will damage more flesh and organs than a small bullet.

Neither school of thought is a guaranteed solution to the stopping power question. At best, all you can hope to do is stack the deck in your favor by making informed, intelligent decisions about weapons, calibers, and their uses.

The main problem with the small-caliber, high-velocity theory is that you simply cannot push a bullet out of a pistol fast enough to guarantee expansion and still provide adequate penetration. It is not enough for the bullet to expand—it must also penetrate deep enough so that the expansion injures something important. Many companies have made considerable amounts of money claiming to have developed the best "mix" balancing these two attributes, and many have come very close. But none has really succeeded. It seems to be easy to develop a bullet that will penetrate deeply and another bullet that will expand broadly. To make a bullet do both things every time has eluded modern science so far.

The low-speed, big-bullet crowd does not rely on wishful expansion. They realize that expansion is a nonissue if they begin with a big bullet of .44/.45 caliber in the first place. The bigger bullet is already causing a greater degree of physical damage than a smaller bullet without relying on the possibility of expansion.

I am not a scientist, and a complete scientific explanation of terminal bullet performance inside human flesh is not the object here. I have, however, seen many people shot with various calibers and have noticed certain things. No pistol caliber is 100 percent reliable in the incapacitation department. The only one-shot stops I have personally seen have been with centerfire rifle cartridges (.308 Winchester) and 12-gauge shotguns (12 pellet 00 buck magnum load). And yes, these can fail as well. There are no guarantees in a gunfight!

Some enterprising scientific types conducted a project

not long ago where goats were shot with various calibers and the results noted for further examination. While an admirable study, the results are still not conclusive with respect to performance on human beings. People usually have psychological reactions to being shot. I have seen people with peripheral wounds convince themselves that being shot was the same as being killed so they simply died. I have also seen a robbery suspect with several "nonsurvivable" wounds so unimpressed with bullet performance that he tried to run over a policeman with his getaway car!

A second variable to consider is what the bullet actually damages once it gets inside the body. A bullet that bypasses all organs and bones and only damages skin and muscle will not do well in stopping the argument. This is where shot placement enters the picture. It isn't enough to simply shoot the adversary somewhere—you must place your shots carefully in a vital area in order to maximize stopping potential. In human beings, this means placing the shots in the thoracic or cranial areas.

This doesn't seem difficult considering the conversational distances at which most shootings occur. It seems even easier when facing the usual static silhouette target at 7 yards on a well-lit shooting range. But it is a different situation at around four o'clock in the morning when the adversary is moving and shooting at you! At such times, you will find that the greatest cause of stopping power failures is, quite simply, missing the target.

A bullet incapacitates its target in two ways. One way is by causing enough blood loss in the adversary to stop him. The other is by damaging the central nervous system (brain or spine). A brain or spine shot is pretty conclusive, with results in the 99 percent bracket even when using a pipsqueak caliber. The problem is that a clean brain shot is difficult for most people to execute, particularly in a stressful situation. An easier proposition is shooting to the "center of mass," aka the chest. This target is substantially larger and easier to hit than the head.

When placing shots into the center of mass, you do not need to punch out the assailant's breast pocket button, nor do you want the shots to be one on top of the other. Two or more hits spread a reasonable distance apart are more realistic and more effective. The reason is simply that the second bullet will not damage what the first bullet has already damaged. A spread of about 4 inches between shots will enhance the insult on the adversary's body and increase the likelihood of incapacitating him.

If after two solid hits the adversary is not interested in going down, more body hits will not convince him. After the body has been hit solidly twice, the nervous system tends to disregard any further injury or pain. Yes, more injury will probably kill the individual . . . eventually. But that is not your objective. Your objective is to incapacitate him—to shut him off and prevent him from killing you or someone else before he dies.

Some well-meaning authorities advise to shoot for the pelvic area in the event of a failure to stop. They theorize that if a man is hit there, he will likely not be able to come after his intended victim. This sounds good on paper when dealing with someone armed with only a contact weapon, but it is clearly suicide when facing an adversary armed with a firearm. Even if it worked as planned and the pelvis shot managed to bring the attacker down, he can still shoot you even if he cannot chase you! If the shot(s) are not successful, you have lost precious time that you could have used more effectively to end the fight. What makes anyone think that if two well-placed shots to the chest didn't interest the man, that a shot in the hips will? Avoid the pelvis shot—it simply doesn't work.

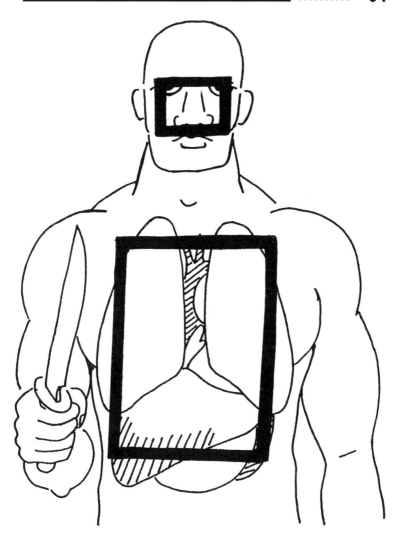

The target zones that will best serve to stop the problem. Plan A is the chest area; plan B is the head.

The answer to a failure to stop is the brain shot. A well-placed shot to the cranial cavity is as close to a guarantee of incapacitation as you can get. Actually doing it after just having shot a man two times without effect is a true test of nerves. And just shooting the adversary in the head is some-times not sufficient. There have been cases of bullets actually glancing off the skull and ricocheting away with no more result than a big bloody gouge. The best policy is to place the shot somewhere in the rectangular "box" that is framed by the eyebrows, upper lip, and corners of the eyes. Ana-tomically speaking, this area is substantially easier to pene-trate than the more armored areas of the skull. Subsequently, any shot that makes it inside the cranial vault will automati-cally disrupt the brain stem and give you the results you seek—a no-reflex kill.

If you have intelligence that the adversary is wearing body armor or is under the influence of drugs, you would be wise to consider the brain shot as plan A and bypass any body shots completely.

In any case, don't just shoot him twice and stand there gawking. Even if you've experienced a failure to stop and have just delivered a brain shot, *keep shooting if he's still moving!* This may mean shooting the head again because the first shot may not have "made it inside." Many supposedly dead crooks have "come back to life" as a hapless policeman stood there wondering why his bullets didn't work.

Consider the possibility of a partially obscured adversary or an adversary who is facing away or at an angle. Taking such a shot is not likely for a private citizen protecting his own life, but it is possible for a policeman sworn to protect others. Shooting an adversary facing 180 degrees away is the same as shooting him straight on at 0 degrees. In this circumstance, the cranial shot is indexed at the central point between the ears. In fact, envision a band about three inches wide around the head that covers the area between eyes and upper lip as well as the ears. That is where the cranial shot is placed for best results.

The target zones from the side are slightly smaller. Notice also that any projectiles may need to penetrate through the arm as well.

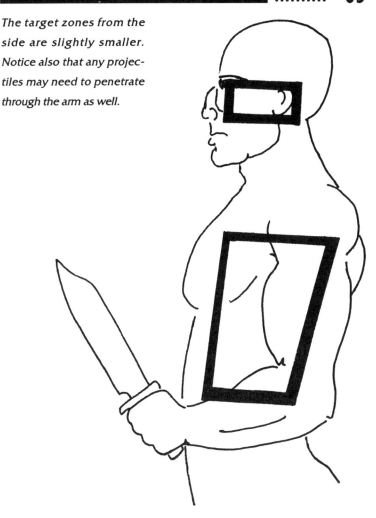

Sometimes an adversary will be at 90 degrees or 270 degrees respectively. Shooting for the center of mass under such circumstances is difficult because of the possibility of an intervening arm. Such a shot will need to penetrate through that arm and still have enough power to make it into the thoracic cavity. Penetration and expansion must be balanced here or the bullet will never reach the vitals.

Incapacitation is influenced by three factors: 1) correct bullet placement to enhance the amount of physical insult and damage to the body; 2) the actual damage accomplished by the bullet, also known as quantity of injury; and 3) the adversary's reaction to being shot. You really only have control over one or at best two of these factors. So practice

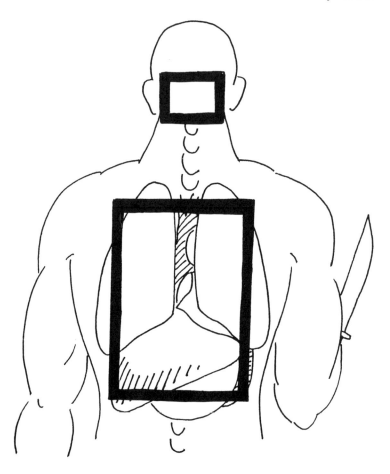

Don't dismiss the notion of shooting a man in the back. For example, what would you do if you saw this goon slithering toward your child's bedroom one warm summer night?

enough to be able to hit that which you wish to hit quickly and under stress, and select a caliber/cartridge that has been proven to succeed most of the time on human beings. Like it or not, this means the big, slow bullet of the .44/.45 school. Carry the biggest gun that you can control.

Some of us are mandated by those that think they know better to carry substandard calibers and ammunition. There is no way around this. Just realize that there is a greater possibility of a failure to stop, and arrange your training accordingly. Whatever the adversary's reaction to your shots will be cannot be predicted or controlled, so be ready to follow up with a cranial shot if the situation calls for such action. Most importantly, remember that there are no guarantees in a gunfight, particularly when it comes to stopping power.

chapter 11

Maintaining Continuity of Fire

SPEED LOAD! The very words conjure images of embattled police officers struggling to recharge their pistols under a hail of criminal gunfire as they desperately try to get back into the fight. In reality, the speed load will seldom be necessary. The rule of thumb regarding reloading is to "reload when you want to, not when you have to." There is a mountain of truth in that statement.

In a gunfight, as in a fistfight, you want to hit your man (or men) as fast and as often as you can. You keep this up until he is no longer a problem. Shooting and hitting are more important than reloading. In fact, the only purpose of reloading is to be able to keep shooting and hitting. Sometimes there is a great urgency to do this.

The IPSC speed load was developed by one of the sport's founders, Ray Chapman. Executing it requires leaving one round in the chamber and jettisoning the empty or partial magazine in order to replace it with a fresh magazine. The reason for retaining the round in the chamber is to allow a shot midstream during the reload if needed. Secondly, it precludes the need to operate the slide release mechanism and, at least in theory, allow a faster reload. The average execution time is 2 seconds (1.5 seconds for an expert). This is a very long time in a gunfight.

During an actual gunfight, it is unlikely that you will be able to keep track of the number of rounds you have fired in order to guarantee that you will leave the mandatory round in the chamber. Additionally, if the fight is still in progress, the need to shoot will supersede the thought of reloading. If any adversary is still on his feet, you would do well to shoot him. If there is one adversary left and one round in the chamber, you should be thinking about shooting, not reloading. The need to reload will probably present itself by surprise—when you are holding an empty gun with the slide locked back.

Even a master gunfighter might run out of ammo if he is faced with more attackers than a full magazine will put down (assuming two or three hits per customer). He might also be re-attacked before he even thinks about reloading. And as much as we try to avoid it, he might even miss. In real life, targets are very difficult to hit because they do not stand tall in the sun as do the paper targets we are accustomed to at the firing range. It may take more shots to put down an enemy than you expected.

In such circumstances, the need to reload will be realized when the pistol will not shoot anymore. A further check will likely reveal that the pistol has not malfunctioned but rather that you have run out of ammo. The act of reloading, therefore, will really be a reaction to the situation—we are reloading when we have to. This is the emergency reload!

Emergency reloading practice must be conducted from a slide-locked, empty-gun position. You want to make the act of releasing the slide and subsequently chambering a round a reflexive action.

The need to reload will probably come as a surprise when the pistol slide locks back during a fight.

Reach for a fresh magazine as you prepare to eject the expended magazine.

Eject the expended magazine as you move the replacement magazine toward the pistol. Let the expended magazine fall to the ground.

Stage the flat portion of the magazine against the flat portion at the back of the magazine well.

Seat it firmly into the magazine well.

As the support hand resumes its position, release the slide and chamber a fresh cartridge.

Back in the fight in about 1.5 seconds!

It is important to realize how it actually "feels" to shoot the last cartridge in the pistol. The recoil forces of the pistol can actually be felt as two separate motions—the rearward motion of extraction/ejection and the forward motion of feeding/chambering. When the last round is fired (when you shoot to "slide lock"), you will only feel the rearward motion because the now empty magazine will activate the slide stop and prevent the subsequent forward motion. This feels different, and you need to commit that feeling to memory and use it as an indicator to trigger the emergency reload response. For those using revolvers, the indication will be a "click" when you expect a "bang."

This is not to imply that you always wait to reload until you are out of ammunition! You still want to reload at a time of your own choosing, behind cover if possible. But it's best to train for the realistic worst possible case.

We proceed from the last shot fired and the pistol on target. Your visual focus moves downrange toward the danger, and it will remain downrange during the execution of the reload. For the semiauto the process is thus. The support hand leaves the pistol and moves to retrieve a magazine (usually from a belt pouch). It is important to wear the spare magazine in the same place at all times. In time you will reflexively reach for that magazine wherever you have programmed yourself to reach for it. The support hand "hits" the magazine bottom with the palm. The fingers then close around it, with the index finger along the front of the magazine. The magazine in the pistol is not released until the replacement magazine is firmly in hand. It is very embarrassing to reach for a magazine that is not there after having ejected the magazine in the pistol.

It is also important to practice drawing the magazine just as you practice drawing the pistol. Note the angle that the magazine is at when it reaches the pistol and rotate the strong hand to match that angle. This will greatly facilitate the insertion of the magazine into the pistol. It is best to keep the pistol pointed toward the target as the existing magazine is ejected. When the fresh magazine reaches the pistol, you want to arrest your speed slightly and let the magazine "coast" into the magazine well. This works much better than trying to muscle it in to save a few tenths of a second. The magazine back meets the back of the magazine well and the palm of the support hand slams it home. The support hand resumes its shooting position after it releases the slide stop, chambering a round as the sights line up again on the target.

The reloading concept does not change for those armed with revolvers, even though the technique is different. The drill begins from the same tactical position as that for the semiauto. The shooting-hand thumb moves to the cylinder release button as the support hand leaves the grip and cradles the revolver at the trigger guard. The support hand's middle fingers contact the cylinder as the firing-hand thumb activates the cylinder release and the cylinder is swung out.

Keeping the weapon at eye level, the shooting hand leaves the revolver and goes to retrieve a speed loader from the belt. Simultaneously, the support hand rotates 180 degrees, inverting the revolver to a barrel-up position as the thumb "pops" the ejector rod sharply, ejecting the spent cases.

Keeping the visual focus downrange, the support hand rotates the revolver to a barrel-down position and brings it toward the body. The firing hand brings the speed loader in line with the cylinder, indexing it with the fingertips. The entire process is facilitated by aligning two rounds with two of the chamber mouths. Doing so automatically aligns the rest of the rounds and is considerably easier than trying to align all six rounds. The best speed loading devices allow an encircling grip with the fingers that hastens the alignment as well as releases the rounds into the cylinder with just a light push.

After releasing the cartridges, close the cylinder with the support hand and reacquire the shooting grip on the way back to the target. Reloading with the revolver is, as you can see, more time consuming.

At other times, there will not be an immediate need to keep shooting. Either the problem will have been solved, or there will be a temporary pause in the fight while everyone regroups. Street fights are very rarely pitched battles; rather, they occur suddenly and end abruptly. But that abrupt end is sometimes just a breather for the attacker, so you must remain on guard even after you think the fight is over.

Part of staying on guard is to avoid standing around with a half-empty gun. There may not be an immediate need to keep shooting, but you want to "top off the tank" in case the war isn't over. There have been many cases of presumably dead criminals "coming back to life" and killing the unwary officers around him. Additionally, you may need to approach the downed attacker or search for his business partners. The

The tactical reload begins by lowering the muzzle enough to be able to see your zone of fire.

Keeping the pistol in position, reach for a replacement magazine with the support hand.

Stage the magazine at the bottom of the magazine well.

Eject the partial magazine and catch it in the palm of the support hand, trapping it between the second and third fingers.

Rotate the support hand clockwise and stage the replacement magazine at the rear of the magazine well.

Seat the replacement magazine.

If the need to shoot occurs at this point, it is a simple matter to reacquire the two-handed grip and still retain the depleted magazine.

If there is no need to shoot, secure the magazine in a pocket for possible later use.

immediate battle may be over, but there may be another battle just seconds away when his backup arrives. It would be tactically imprudent to meet them with only a partially loaded pistol.

This is what is meant by loading when you want to—the "tactical reload." You proceed from a muzzle depressed position (just low enough to be able to see the target, not lower). The pistol remains cocked and off safe. The trigger finger leaves the trigger guard and the support hand retrieves a magazine from the magazine pouch in the same fashion as for the emergency reload. The support-hand palm comes to a stop at the floorplate of the magazine in the pistol. The strong-hand thumb presses the magazine release button and releases the magazine halfway onto the support-hand palm. The magazine is captured between the second and third fingers of the support hand, fully extracted, and retained in that location during the maneuver. The support hand rotates toward the pistol, bringing the fresh magazine into alignment with the magazine well. The support hand then inserts the fresh magazine into the magazine well and seats it into the pistol. If you need to, you can begin firing now.

In an emergency, you can immediately reestablish the grip and begin shooting. In such a case, the partial magazine remains "trapped" where it is during any subsequent action because the need to shoot precludes the risk of dropping or losing the partial magazine. In the event of a subsequent need for an emergency reload, the magazine between the fingers can be used to recharge the pistol and keep shooting.

If there is no immediate threat at the conclusion of the tactical reload, the support hand can simply stash the magazine into a pocket, waistband, etc. Just don't put it back into the magazine case, where you might later mistake it for a fully loaded one!

The tactical reload for a revolver involves replacing the spent cases with cartridges and requires the use of a loop carrier. The weapon is lowered enough to be able to see the target. The weapon's trigger guard is placed in the support-hand palm. The shooting hand actuates the cylinder release as the support hand's second and third fingers push "through" the frame, opening the cylinder and holding it in place. The index and little finger are placed over the top of

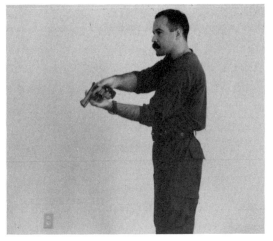

Revolver shooters use different techniques, but the concepts remain the same. The need to emergency reload will be a indicated by a "click" instead of a "bang." Bring the pistol off the target and open the cylinder with the support hand.

Pivot the pistol so the muzzle is pointing up, punch the ejector rod with the support hand, and eject the spent cases. At the same time, reach for and secure the speedloader on the belt.

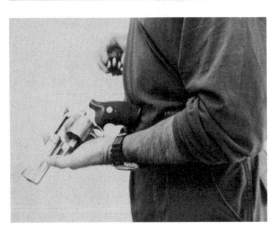

Index the pistol butt against the belly and stage the speedloader with the strong hand.

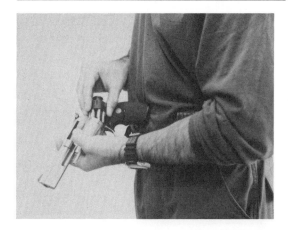

Index two bullet tips into the chambers (the other bullet tips will be aligned automatically this way).

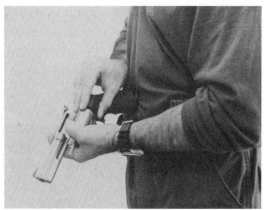

Activate the speedloader and release the cartridges into the cylinder.

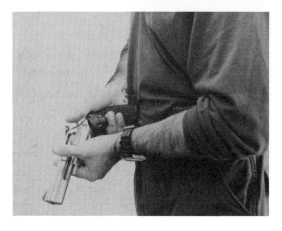

Ignoring the now empty speedloader, begin to close the cylinder.

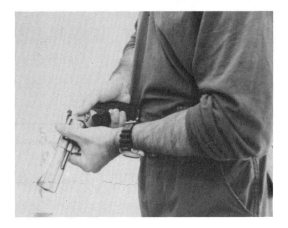

Close the cylinder and get back into the fight.

the frame to prevent movement. Using the support thumb, raise the ejector rod about 1/3 to 1/2 its normal travel, remove the spent cases with the shooting hand two at a time, and discard them. Reload the same way, two at a time. Now close the cylinder and get back on target.

When practicing, you shouldn't integrate these techniques as part of a shooting drill. For example, it is common to see advanced shooters conducting a "shoot two/reload/shoot two" drill. This will undoubtedly program the shooter to reload needlessly after only two rounds have been

The tactical reload for the revolver follows the same concept as that for the autoloading pistol. Begin by opening the cylinder with the support hand and staging the ejector rod.

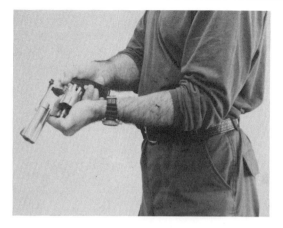

Depress the ejector rod and note the position of the cases with spent primers.

Extract the spent cases two at a time and discard them.

Secure the replacement cartridges two at a time and . . .

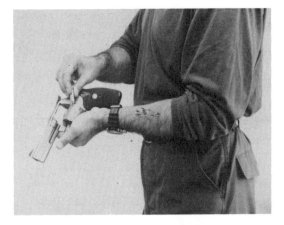

. . . insert them into the cylinder.

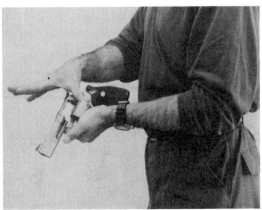

Be certain that they are seated fully into the chambers.

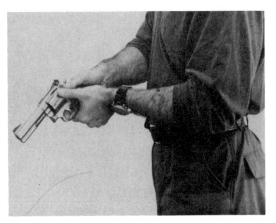

Close the cylinder. Tactical reload completed.

fired. It is possible that he will do just that in a fight because that is what he has trained himself to do. A better way is to practice reloading drills separate from shooting drills.

Both emergency and tactical reloads can be conducted on the move, but it is best to be well hidden behind cover if you need to fiddle with your weapon. The tactical reload occurs at a time of your choosing, so you can always execute it from a covered position. The emergency reload may catch you in the open, but if you are not shooting, you should be moving to cover. Move, shoot, move to cover, reload, shoot again!

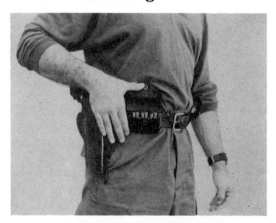

The 2 x 2 x 2" tactical reload pouch holds the cartridges by twos, facilitating their efficient retrieval.

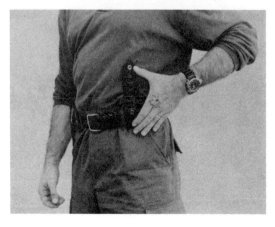

This type of pouch holds the speed-loader onto the belt by straddling the belt and facilitates retrieving the loader. The author's preference in speed-loaders—the Safariland CompII.

Approach the practice of these two techniques in the same manner as training the presentation. Continuous repetition will make both techniques reflexive. It has been said that it is better to solve the tactical problem with the top half of the magazine than the bottom half. I agree completely. The odds are that you will be able to sort out your attackers with less than half the capacity of your pistol's magazine. But odds, like luck, are fickle and unpredictable. These two methods of maintaining continuity of fire will keep you ready when they are against you.

Clearing Pistol Malfunctions

Without question, one of the most desirable attributes of a fighting pistol is reliability. But contrary to many manufacturer's claims, no pistol is 100 percent reliable. Anything man-made can fail, quite often at very inopportune times. Knowing this, it is important to learn and understand immediate action drills for clearing weapons malfunctions rapidly as well as knowing how to minimize their occurrence.

Most pistol malfunctions are caused by defective magazines or defective ammunition or are operator induced. The best courses of action to ensure reliable function are to use quality magazines and ammunition as well as have a relatively clean weapon. Magazines should be examined periodically for minor cracks, proper spring tension, and the condition of the feed lips at the top. Suspect magazines should be so marked and relegated to the practice range, never to be carried on the street again. Ammunition carried in a fighting pistol should be checked for function in that particular pistol before being carried for defense. These two actions will help minimize the possibility of encountering functioning problems.

Operator-induced malfunctions are another thing altogether and can only be prevented by having a thorough understanding of the functioning cycle of your particular pistol.

Each malfunction will have a direct cause, but the middle of a fight is no place for a diagnosis. The following malfunction clearing drills will allow you to recognize the characteristics of each malfunction, decide which type it is, conduct actions to clear it, and bring the weapon back into the fight. It is important to know the indication for each type of malfunction to avoid prolonged analysis of how to clear it during a shoot-out. It is also important to maintain the weapon at eye level during the clearance drills both to save precious time and to be able to keep a peripheral eye downrange.

Position One Malfunction

A "position one" malfunction is a failure to fire. The indication is simply that you get a "click" when you expect a "bang." This may be caused by a defective cartridge, a broken firing pin, or an unseated magazine. With weapons such as the Smith & Wesson pistols equipped with magazine disconnectors, you will have an inoperative trigger as well if the magazine is not fully seated. The clearance drill is to tap the magazine floorplate sharply with the heel of the weak hand to ensure it is seated properly and then quickly cycle the slide while flipping the pistol horizontally to the right to eject the defective round. If this does not bring the pistol back into action, repeat the process. If the subsequent attempt doesn't solve the problem, you probably have a broken firing pin and a tactical retreat is in order.

Position Two Malfunction

A "position two" malfunction is a failure to eject—the classic "stovepipe." This can be caused by a defective maga-

The existence of a failure to fire will be evident when you get a "click" instead of a "bang." The solution is a TAP to the bottom of the magazine.

Step two is to FLIP the pistol to the strong side.

Step three is to sharply RACK the slide to the rear and . . .

. . . let it return into battery, chambering a fresh cartridge.

Back on target in about 1 to 1.5 seconds.

zine that interferes with the ejection process or by a broken or weakened extractor or ejector. A recoil spring that is too strong for the particular ammunition may also contribute to the problem. The indication that a P-2 malfunction has occurred is a brass case protruding from the ejection port. The trigger will also be inoperative because the slide will be out of battery. The immediate action drill is identical to that for the P-1 malfunction.

The original drill for clearing a P-2 malfunction was to sweep the hand over the top of the slide, striking the protruding brass case and both ejecting it and chambering a new cartridge. Many of today's pistol designs feature slide-mounted decocking levers that may be activated inadvertently by sweeping the hand over the slide. Additionally, many of these same designs don't exhibit an obviously protruding brass case to latch on to in the case of a P-2. The "tap/rack/flip" easily solves both the P-1 and P-2 malfunctions quickly and effectively, regardless of the weapon used. Using one drill to solve two problems keeps things simpler and more efficient.

Position Three Malfunction

A "position three" malfunction is a feedway stoppage caused by a failure to eject the spent case, which obstructs the feeding of the next round. This is the most serious type of mal-

The failure to eject or stovepipe will be indicated when you see brass protruding from the ejection port instead of the front sight. Additionally, the slide will be out of battery and the trigger will be inoperative. The solution to the problem is the same as for the failure to fire. Begin with a TAP!

FLIP!

RACK!

Let the slide return to battery and get back on target. You're back in the fight in 1 to 1.5 seconds.

The feedway stoppage (position three malfunction) will be evident when the slide is substantially out of battery and the trigger is inoperative. Further investigation will reveal brass in the ejection port. Step one is to LOCK the slide to the rear.

STRIP out the existing magazine and discard it.

RACK the slide two to three times to clear out any trash in the ejection/feedway area.

Retrieve a fresh magazine and stage it by the magazine well.

Seat the magazine (TAP).

RACK the slide and chamber a fresh cartridge.

Back in the fight in 4 to 5 seconds.

function because it takes the most time to clear. The P-3 indications are a slide that is considerably out of battery and an inoperative trigger. This will feel differently than shooting to a slide-lock position. Think of the recoil cycle as two distinct movements of back and forward. An empty magazine that locks back the slide on the last shot will only let you experience half that cycle (the rearward portion). The P-3 will allow you to experience the rearward cycle and about half the forward cycle (about three quarters of a full recoil cycle). Knowing how this feels will help minimize the time to decide whether you are holding an empty gun or if you've had a P-3.

The solution for a P-1 or P-2 can be executed in an instant, but the P-3 takes much longer. This means that when you recognize a P-3, your first thought must be to *get behind cover now!* The P-3 will require about four seconds to clear—long enough to get shot several times. This is an eternity in a gunfight that lasts two to three seconds, and you do not want to stand around in the kill zone.

To solve a P-3 malfunction, first lock back the slide to relieve the spring pressure on the magazine and the trapped cartridges. Then strip the magazine out of the pistol using the last two fingers of the support hand. (The reason you use only the last two fingers is because they are the only fingers that will be available if you encounter a "stuck" magazine during a reloading procedure. You want to do as many things as possible using the same techniques to minimize terminal confusion.) Note that this may take some effort since the first cartridge may be hung up on the feed ramp. Since in all likelihood the magazine was the cause of the problem, discard it once you've gotten it out. Now cycle the slide vigorously several times to clear out any remaining cases or cartridges. The pistol is now clear but also quite empty, so obtain a fresh magazine from your belt and insert it quickly into the pistol, followed by one final cycle of the slide to chamber a fresh cartridge.

Position Four Malfunction

A "position four" malfunction is simply a slide that fails to go into battery. Unless the pistol is extremely dirty, the cause is probably an oversized cartridge. In the former case, a light rap on the back of the slide will usually close it. If this doesn't do the trick, revert back to the fix for position one and two malfunctions.

These four immediate-action drills will solve most malfunctions you might encounter with a semiauto pistol. There are other possible malfunctions proprietary to particular pistols. The firing pin stop on the 1911 .45 pistol, for example, may work loose and cause a stoppage. The slide-mounted decocking levers on the S&W and Beretta 92F pistols may suffer from weakened springs and activate during recoil. Finally, the complicated mechanisms of the revolver may become fouled up and render it inoperative. In direct contrast to the self-loading pistol, the malfunctioning revolver often requires the use of tools to fix. This, in reality, takes its operator out of the fight unless he has access to a second pistol.

These drills can be perfected with inert ammunition during dry firing practice. The best option is to follow regular weapon maintenance, carry proven magazines, and check out duty ammunition for fit and function. But like a spare tire in the trunk or a parachute on an airplane, malfunction clearance drills are a nice thing to have for life's unexpected emergencies.

The Rules of Close-Quarters Combat

A pistol may be needed to solve a problem that presents itself across the street, but it will more likely be needed to solve a problem across a table. The defensive nature of the

When moving in extreme close quarters or in crowded tactical situations, keeping the pistol in the weapon-retention position is the best option.

pistol dictates that it will generally be used for close-range problems. Long-range problems are not defensive in nature and, when expected, are better handled with more suitable weapons.

Rule One

Rule one of close-quarters combat: *maximize the distance from a potential threat in order to minimize your exposure to it!* This is a fine idea, and in a perfect world you would always know that trouble was on the menu before the appetizers were served! Alas, most of us do not live in a perfect world, and oftentimes we find ourselves within handshake distances of questionable persons.

Along with your standard shooting skills, you need to study the problem at the tag-you're-it distances of everyday urban life (which, by the way, are much closer than the standard 7-yard line). Typical stats for gunfights tell us that when quarters get close, they get close indeed—like within 5 feet! The reaction time for an average man is about 1/4 second. This is the time that will elapse even before a decision is made to draw

The "speed rock"—refined for combative use by Chuck Taylor—is a last-option technique for arm's-length situations where there is no room to evade or maneuver.

The shooter "rocks" the pistol out of the holster and simultaneously "rocks" his torso back to bring the muzzle onto the adversary's vital zone.

the pistol. If your adversary is standing within 5 feet and decides to draw and shoot you, you will be at least a quarter second behind in your reaction. This means that whoever initiates the action usually wins, because the other party's reaction will always be too slow (when within arm's reach). Even if you are well practiced, when you are close enough to smell your opponent's bad breath, the best you can hope for is that you will shoot each other almost simultaneously!

Rule Two

Rule two of close-quarters combat: *he who moves first will usually win—so be "offsides" on the play!*

Try this experiment. Secure a training partner and venture to the pistol range. With holstered pistols, you will each draw and shoot a target placed 10 feet downrange. Have your partner initiate the drill by drawing and shooting first. As you glimpse him moving toward his gun in your peripheral vision, draw your own weapon and shoot your own target as fast as you can. Your partner will probably get his shot off before you do, but the two shots will be remarkably close. Use a shooting timer to illustrate the point.

The preceding drill will demonstrate that your shot will follow your partner's by less than half a second. This means that if you both shoot at each other within arm's length, you will both be shot, albeit one will die less than a half second before the other. Who really wins here? Nobody. If you must let an adversary tip his hand, as you must often do in defensive situations, you want to do something to forestall his ability to hit you. You need to do more than just move first if you can to buy that quarter to half second necessary to get your own weapon out and working. That brings us to the third rule.

Rule Three

Rule three of close-quarters combat: *move as you shoot, move after you shoot!* Then move to a position of cover. If you expect trouble, move to a covered position before it starts.

Moving and shooting may be difficult at long distances, but it is relatively easy at the back-slapping range of 5 feet or less. We are not talking about dancing a jig during a firing string. A quick sidestep on the draw will do. Sidesteps are preferable over stepping back because a sidestep may take you out of the way of the bad guy's muzzle as he draws, whereas a backstep will not.

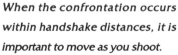

When the confrontation occurs within handshake distances, it is important to move as you shoot.

Generally, it is better to move to the adversary's strong side and stay to the back of his gun hand. His shot may only miss you by inches, but if you stand still, it may not miss you at all.

You may even want to sidestep to one side rather than another. The reason is that when a person presents his pistol to shoot, he does so in a directional line to where he has perceived the target to be. Such a ballistic motion is nearly impossible to change and redirect midstream, and it is more difficult to redirect it to the strong side than the support side. Redirecting to the support side is more natural because it "follows" the existing motion of the draw. Redirecting to the strong side goes against that motion. This is similar to the act of throwing a baseball right-handed into a catcher's mitt across the yard at the 12 o'clock. Mid-throw it is possible to redirect the throw with some effort to the 9 o'clock but much more difficult to redirect to the 3 o'clock.

This means that if you move to the opponent's strong side and stay on the backside of the gun hand, it will be more difficult for him to "track" you with his muzzle than if you move to his support side. I am not suggesting that it is possible to dodge bullets, but getting out of the way of a "draw" motion might keep you from getting shot. And make no mistake—moving to either side is much more preferable to standing still.

If you are close enough, slapping his gun away might be an option as you move and draw.

How do you determine your opponent's strong or

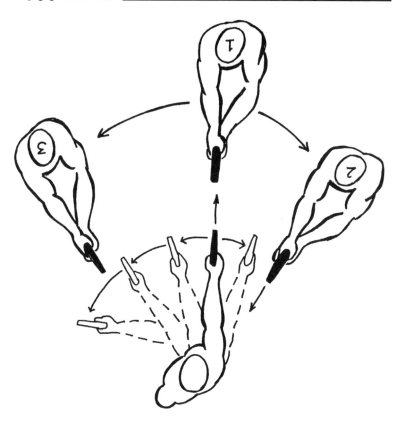

Moving to the opponent's support side (illustrated by figure 3) will allow him to track you with his muzzle. This will be more markedly difficult for him to do if you move to his strong side and stay to the back of his gun hand (illustrated by figure 2).

support side? Look at where his pistol is carried and how. Most people will carry the pistol in a manner to allow the strong hand access to the butt. You might also notice the placement of rings and watches, since most people will traditionally place these items on particular sides. Also, the strong hand will probably be the first one that moves for the pistol when the fight starts.

Sometimes a shot will be required when the background is less than ideal, causing concern about overpenetration. Angling the shot upward will help minimize problems with overpenetration. A simple squatting motion will angle the shots 30 to 45 degrees upward.

Sometimes you will be in extremely crowded situations where there will be no room to maneuver, such as on stairs, in narrow hallways, or in the midst of uninvolved personnel (sometimes called innocent bystanders). A secondary concern here is that overpenetrating or (horrors!) missed rounds will strike things other than the intended target. You can minimize the latter by moving downward and angling the shots upward into the bad guy. This can be done by dropping quickly into a high kneel or squatting position as you shoot.

If no movement is possible and you are within arm's reach of the adversary, you can aggress forward and either pin his gun hand against his body or actually pull yourself around to his strong side using his own body as a shield. During these maneuvers, you will of course be bringing your own pistol into action for contact shots against the adversary's vital and available zones. This is where hand-to-hand combat and pistolcraft merge. The closer you get to the adversary, the closer to your body you must keep your pistol. At the interval of actual physical contact, you will be shooting from a weapon-retention position and almost making contact with your muzzle against the assailant's body. This is the most dangerous interval because even an inept, clumsy fighter can get lucky and cause you terminal problems. You do not want to spend much time that close. Hit him hard and keep hitting him as you extract to a safer distance or, far better, to a covered position.

It is important to realize some things particular to the use of pistols at contact distances. The destruction of tissue from a contact gunshot wound will be remarkably enhanced due to the expanding and burning gases that will enter the body along with the projectile. It is important to know that some semiauto pistols of the Colt/Browning type will unlock when pressed against an attacker's body and will not fire. This means that you should keep the muzzle slightly back from actual contact. Also, you will find that flesh and blood are often ejected out through the entry wound due to the massive force created by the expanding gases. This ejected meat can gum up the pistol substantially, preventing follow-up shots. This last phenomena will be less likely if the shot is placed on a clothed part of the body, as the clothing will generally retain the blood and tissue. (This may be a grisly and unpleasant topic of discussion, but it's a necessary one. Forewarned is forearmed!)

Rule Four

Rule four of close-quarters combat: *use distractions to precede your actions whenever possible!*

An undercover associate of mine who goes around in baggy clothes with his baseball cap turned sideways relates that he was "working" a drug case involving a particularly nasty group of criminals. During one assignment, he was suddenly faced up-close with a belligerent goon conspicuously sporting a pistol stuck in his belt at the "belly button" position. Thinking quickly, my friend threw his untouched rum and Coke into the gorilla's eyes, distracting him, and snatched the bad guy's pistol out of the belt himself! The rest

Assaults are often preceded by nonphysical clues.

If such an assault is imminent, you can preempt it with a distraction. Then move and shoot as necessary.

of the story had a happy ending . . . but not for the bad guy.

This was quite a desperate situation, but quick thinking and decisiveness won out. Distractions are designed to take your adversary's mind momentarily off the notion of shooting you by making him think of something else. That something else could be the car keys flying at him, the scorching hot coffee dripping down his face, or the pen protruding from his eye! Think about it awhile and you'll likely come up with more inventive and effective distraction techniques.

Just as you use diversion and maneuver to your advantage, it can be turned against you if you're not careful. Once you have the initiative of offense, you must retain it until you have flattened your man or hurt him enough so that you can execute a tactical withdrawal and "get out of Dodge." This leads to rule five.

Rule Five

Rule five of close-quarters combat: *the more violent you become in a fight, the less violent the adversary will become!* This can be taken to a point dictated by your particular rules of engagement.

Remember why you are shooting this man—because he will kill you if you do not put him down. You cannot assume that your bullets will stop him with one or two shots, so keep hitting him until he is down and out of the picture. If you must precede your shooting with a strike of some sort, make it with conviction. This is no time for sentiment, civility, or political correctness. Fight hard!

Other thoughts relating to close-quarters combat:

Weapon Retention

No discussion of close combat would be complete without addressing the issue of weapon retention. This problem appears in two forms: the adversary either attempts to snatch your gun out of the holster (presumably by surprise) or he gloms onto the already drawn pistol in an attempt to wrest it out of your hand.

Let's examine the first instance, the holstered pistol. There is a plethora of gadget holsters designed to be snatchproof life-savers or your money back. *They are not a substitute for an alert mind!* Weapon retention is not a technical issue, it is a mental issue. Weapon retention is best solved with an alert

If you don't pay attention to the pistol on your belt, somebody else will!

countenance and a proper mind-set. As the fighter pilots say, "Check your six." You cannot take a pistol away from a man who is expecting trouble. Avoid holsters that unnecessarily hinder the drawing process. A simple thumb break design for a uniform holster and a cautious attitude will suffice.

With nonuniform or concealment holsters, retention devices are optional since a weapon that's not in plain view will not be an invitation to a snatch attempt. This is clearly an individual choice. My concealment holster has no such retention device. In any case, it is unwise to rely on equipment alone to retain the pistol.

Keep the gun side away from all contacts, and be aware that someone may attempt to take it from you!

The primary thing to remember is to keep your gun side away from questionable people. Many goons will try to snatch your pistol if they have the opportunity. Don't give them the chance.

At the police academy some years ago, we were taught to be extremely gun-conscious by our drill instructors. At the most inopportune moments, they would reach out and try to snatch our unloaded handguns from our holsters. Pity the unfortunate cadet who did not anticipate this and take instant countermeasures. This all

Simply keeping the strong-side elbow positioned over the holstered pistol may forestall a gun grab.

served to produce an almost palpable sensitivity to any-thing near our holstered weapons. This can be likened to the wallet-sensitive alertness that you might feel while walking through a crowd of pickpockets. It is condition yellow at its best. Those who wear pistols on a daily basis cannot let their attention lapse when they are around unfamiliar people. Pistol-conscious sensitivity is paramount. Develop it!

Know this: in most situations where a pistol is snatched, it will be used against the snatchee. Someone glomming onto your pistol, whether in the holster or in the hand, is a serious matter indeed, and you are justified in dealing with him harshly enough to use as deadly a force as you can muster to retain your weapon. This is no time for "verbal judo" or futile "control" holds.

If the pistol is still holstered when hostile hands reach for it, you need to pin the adversary's hands in place and hold the pistol into the holster with all your will. Once you are cer-tain that the pistol has at least been stabilized, you can attempt countermeasures against the grabber.

Gun grabs will not generally be announced by your adversary, so stay alert.

If it does occur, the first step is to SECURE the pistol.

The most effective methods are those involving the principles of leverage. These methods use the full weight of the body against the grabber's hand, wrist, or arm to provide the leverage to peel the offending hand off the holstered pistol.

A large percentage of disarmed individuals are killed with their own weapons, so you are justified in taking a gun-grab attempt badly. The back-up gun may be a wise option in such cases.

Once the gun is "clear" and a safe distance has been achieved, you can begin to deal with him effectively. Let your conscience be your guide.

If the pistol is out when it is grabbed, you must do whatever is necessary to get the muzzle pointing toward the gun grabber. This accomplished, you then literally blow him off the end of the gun. This will work to varying degrees depending on the particular weapon involved. For example, a revolver can be readily made inoperative by clamping down hard on the cylinder, thereby precluding the necessary rotation that must occur prior to firing. Similarly, a double-action pistol or revolver can be prevented from firing by gripping around and pinning down the hammer. It would be unwise to rely on these mechanical tricks alone, but when coupled with strong basic techniques, they may provide you with that extra second that you need.

If you find that the pistol will not shoot, then you must relinquish one hand to produce a second weapon (back-up

If your daily attire includes a pistol, you must realize that you cannot afford to lose a single physical encounter.

Be prepared to do whatever it takes to win because if you do not, your opponent will soon be armed . . . with your gun!

There are other options besides using the pistol. Here we see that the pen is mightier than the sword. Use your imagination!

gun, knife, ball point pen, etc.) or use the empty hand for some distraction therapy to the adversary's most exposed vitals, followed by a leverage technique to recover full control of the pistol.

Dealing with Contact Weapons

Not every goon who crosses your path will be armed with the latest model service pistol. Encountering knives is a far greater likelihood than you might at first believe. Many pistoleros, for example (yours truly included), often carry one or two utility blades to augment their more powerful weapons. For some criminal types, the blade is preferred. In their eyes, knives are cheap, easily disposed of, untraceable, and deadly effective. Remember that a well-trained, proficient bladesman may still be able to conduct all manner of exploratory surgery on you even after you've shot him full of magic bullets. For those nonbelievers out there, I suggest perusing the history of the American/Filipino unpleasantness of the previous century.

Some might argue that within arm's reach, the blade is the equal of the pistol. To escape the pistol you need only evade the muzzle. Not so with the knife, since it not only has a point but also an edge or two. The utility of the knife decreases as you increase the distance. Circus knife throwers aside, a knife is effective at arm's length but not across the room. If your man winds up to throw the blade at a distance greater than arm's length, deal with him the same as if he were drawing a pistol. Move as you shoot and move after you shoot.

Some years ago, a noted police instructor determined that the interval for a bladesman to cover 7 yards and cut his target was approximately the same as that for a shooter to draw and fire his pistol. The cut and the shot were often simultaneous. Remember our discussion on reaction times and close combat. Nothing has changed here. You must create all the distance you can. You must place obstacles between you and the bladesman in order to make his charge difficult. Above all, you must avoid closing with him unless it is unavoidable. The instant the adversary begins to move toward you, it becomes a deadly force situation. Shoot him.

Use of Pistols as Contact Weapons

Some authorities advocate using the pistol as a contact weapon to club the adversary. Such activities are not recommended unless you've shot your pistol empty, lost your spare magazines, lost your back-up pistol, lost your knife, and are too physically feeble or wounded to hit him with your hands. I have a friend who got into a serious discussion about the virtues of the criminal justice system with a burglar one night and decided to give him a SIG-Sauer across the melon to quiet him down. The impact of the blow half-cycled his slide, partially ejecting the chambered round and creating a feedway stoppage. The blow did manage to send the burglar on a high-speed trip to dreamland, but had our friend needed to shoot the burglar's business partner, his gun would not have worked.

Facing a Drawn Pistol (or Shoulder Weapon)

If you find yourself in the unenviable position where the criminal has "the drop" on you, you are in a bad way indeed! But all is not lost. Trying a desperate move and getting killed beats getting killed without trying anything at all. The desperate move might work, and, after all, you have nothing to lose at this point.

Remember that whoever moves first will generally win. The three most important issues in such situations are to 1) move first, using surprise to your benefit; 2) shift the centerline of the body away and out of line with the muzzle of his weapon; and 3) seize and control the gun hand (or barrel if it is a shoulder weapon). All three things must be done simultaneously. After this is done, you can move into a leverage technique to rip the weapon away from your assailant or, if you can pull it off, draw your own pistol and shoot him. Realize that this is a desperate situation, but it is far preferable to a desperate execution!

Whatever eventuality may present itself at arm's length, when you begin shooting, do not stop at one or two shots. Move as you shoot, move after you shoot. Use distractions to cover your attack. When the fight starts, be violent! Shoot in "hammers" (very quick pairs), one after the other. Shoot two shots to the chest first, then shoot for the head. Repeat as necessary. In this age of chemical dependency, ballistic t-shirts, and puny cartridges, it's difficult to trust any caliber/bullet/load to provide a conclusive end to the discussion. So keep hitting him until he is more down than the price of sand in Arabia. Then extract, still shooting if necessary, to a position of cover and shoot again if he's still not impressed. Keep these things in mind for those close encounters of the deadly kind.

chapter 14

Long Shots

The vast majority of gunfights will occur within arm's reach, but a full 15 percent seem to take place beyond 50 feet. Therefore, it is important to conduct at least 15 percent of your practice at that distance and beyond. Such long-range shooting problems demand more precision than speed, and you can generally afford to spend a few seconds to take the shot. This means that you should adopt a supported position if you can. It also means that you must pay particular attention to the basics of marksmanship—much more closely than when you are shooting a target at arm's length.

The quickest supported shooting position is kneeling. A kneeling position can be assumed in a couple of seconds and evacuated just as quickly. This position facilitates the use of cover and is useful if vegetation or terrain obscure target visibility. This last attribute is very important when what is obscuring the target is too high to use a prone position.

To adopt a kneeling position quickly, pivot on the ball of the strong-side foot as the strong hand obtains a firing grip on the pistol and the support hand takes its position in front of the left pectoral muscle. The support-side foot steps across

To assume the kneeling position, step across the centerline with the support-side foot as you reach for the pistol.

Lower the entire body until the strong-side buttock rests on the strong-side heel.

Rest the flat portion of the support-side elbow on the flat portion of the support-side knee above the knee-cap. This is a solid and stable position.

an imaginary line projecting from the strong-side foot to the target. Now as the weapon is drawn from the holster, simply sit down on the strong-side foot. As the strong-side knee hits the deck, the strong-side buttock sits on the strong-side heel and the flat portion of the supporting elbow is placed on the flat portion of the support-side knee, above the kneecap. It is important to maintain the support-side elbow vertical for side-to-side stability.

When the terrain and cover allow its use, the prone position is best. The prone position, or more correctly the rollover prone, was developed during the old days of IPSC by Ray Chapman. It allows you to exploit more of the accuracy potential of your weapon than any other shooting position. Many knowledgeable shooters use this same position to sight in their pistols.

To assume the rollover prone position, begin facing the

An alternative to the kneeling position is the squatting position. Simply squat down like an Olympic power-lifter as low as possible until the buttocks rest on the backs of the calves.

Rest the flat portion of the support elbow on the flat portion of the knee above the kneecap.

The prone position is the most stable shooting platform of all. To assume it, drop to both knees as you reach for the holstered pistol.

Break the fall with your support side and begin moving the pistol toward the target.

target and pivot about 45 degrees to the strong side and then obtain the grip on the pistol with the strong hand while the support hand takes its place in front of the support-side pectoral muscle while you drop to your knees. As you draw the pistol from the holster, thrust the torso forward and break your fall with the support hand. Maintaining your forward

Thrust the pistol toward the target and lower the body down onto the strong side.

Reacquire the grip and draw the support-side knee up toward the stomach. Solid, stable, and on target!

direction, thrust the pistol toward the target and lower yourself onto your strong side. The support hand is brought to the weapon for a rested two-handed hold and the support-side leg is drawn up toward the abdomen. Some shooters favor crossing the support-side foot across the strong-side knee. Both of these last points hold the body up on its side, taking pressure off the breathing process and preventing the breathing from affecting the sight picture.

Both these positions will assist in stabilizing your long-range shots, but you must pay extra attention to your sights to make those distant shots. The sights should be adjusted so that the shots will hit directly above the spot where you superimpose the front sight. Your visual focus must be exclusively and sharply on the front sight. Under field conditions, your focus will likely shift back and forth from sight to target, but your *final* focus must be on the front sight when you break the shot.

As much as you try to steady the pistol, you will experience some movement of the sights. This will be more pronounced in the kneeling position than in the prone. Realize that no one can hold a pistol completely still. What you can do, however, is continually strive to keep the sights aligned with each other and push them toward the place that you want to hit. Horizontal and vertical sight movement represents changing angles of the pistol barrel. Changing the angle of the barrel relative to the target represents a miss out at the target. The more distant the target, the smaller that angle must be to secure a hit. If your sights are aligned perfectly with each other, however, your hands (and consequently the pistol) can move a considerable amount and still be on target. Theoretically, your perfectly aligned sights can move within a 4-inch circle and still fire a 4-inch group at 50 yards. You must hold that alignment before, during, and after the shot.

The chances of requiring a long-distance shot are slim for the armed citizen but are becoming more common for the policeman. In either case, do not limit yourself to shooting at conversational distances alone.

chapter

Cover and Concealment

(Previously published in *Soldier of Fortune* magazine, May 1993, under the title "Cover and Concealment.")

The concepts of cover and concealment are vital in a gunfight. If you use them properly, they can protect you from hostile gunfire and give you a base from which to mount an assault. If you use these tactics negligently, they can cost you the element of surprise, the advantage of protection, and maybe your life.

Cover and concealment are two separate issues. Cover can sometimes serve as concealment, but not the reverse. Seeking cover to the exclusion of all other alternatives is never advisable. Neither one, by itself, is the universal solution to the problems of a firefight.

Cover provides protection from gunfire as well as possible concealment of your location. The former attribute is the more important of the two. When thinking of cover, think of solid objects that are likely to resist bullets. Things like brick walls, vehicle engine compartments, telephone poles, and fire hydrants make good cover.

Concealment provides visual deception but not ballistic protection. A concealed position will not allow you to trade shots with an adversary. It will give you a base from which to

Concealment provides a place to hide but no ballistic protection.

launch an unexpected and unannounced assault (yes, that means an ambush). Concealment demands silence and stillness. Sometimes this is all that is needed. If the adversary doesn't know where you are, he won't generally think to shoot at you.

Cover is anything with a high probability for absorbing or deflecting incoming bullets. Here a shooter uses the engine compartment of his vehicle for cover.

Concealment can only be used prior to a confrontation to launch an unexpected assault or to remain hidden and overlooked. Cover, on the other hand, can be used at all times since it can provide for the attributes of concealment as well as protection from gunfire during the fight. If you have a choice in the matter, choosing cover is preferable to choosing concealment only.

To use cover, you need three specific conditions. First, there must be enough *time* to reach cover safely. Second, there must be enough *distance* between you and the hostile to allow the time required to move to cover. Time and distance are inseparably linked. The closer a threat is to you the less time you have to react to it. Conversely, the farther away a threat is the more time available. Finally, you must *anticipate* that a fight is imminent. If you don't think that you are going to have to fight *right now*, it really won't matter how much time or distance you have available because you will probably be surprised by the attack. All three elements must be present or the tactic of seeking cover does not fit the situation.

Some gunfight tacticians and shooting instructors advise to always seek cover regardless of the situation. In the same breath, they condemn the "John Wayne" types who stand up and simply shoot it out with the bad guys. While neither concept is the final answer, a realistic analysis of the circumstances must be done. If you actually have time to think about what is going on instead of simply reacting reflexively, you probably have time to seek cover.

In close range, however, confrontations occur unexpectedly and very quickly. Do you really think that the notion of jumping behind cover will even occur to anyone under such circumstances? In reality, shooting and killing the other fellow before he does the same to you is probably a more prudent plan.

Don't misunderstand; I'm not advocating against using cover if the situation allows it, but at the tag-you're-it distances of most gunfights, a quick and devastating counterattack will work better.

When the distances increase, so does your time interval to react. But don't relax yet. Greater distances may also mean that more powerful weapons such as a rifle or shotgun could be involved. Now the issues of cover and concealment take on greater significance. Such scenarios are much more complex since the weapons involved are capable of more diverse roles.

Regardless of the distance involved in the initial assault, if you don't have time to seek cover when the fight begins, by all means get behind it as soon as is tactically possible! Similarly, any reloading or malfunction clearing should be done behind cover. Once "covered," stay there.

There are reasons to leave cover. One is to prevent being outflanked by an adversary. That means that the adversary is trying to maneuver to a location where he can bypass your cover and shoot into your position. If you realize this is taking place and cannot prevent it with gunfire, you must move to a new covered position to cancel out his tactic. A second reason to leave cover is to press your own assault or to attempt the same tactic of flanking the adversary.

Why not simply increase the distance between you and the threat, thereby allowing the use of cover? Realistically this is possible only when you anticipate the fight, at which point you can simply step behind something solid without much fanfare, just in case.

Why not simply run to cover while returning fire? When dealing with the short time frame/short distance scenario, you need immediate termination of the threat. The more time he has to shoot at you, the more likely he is to hit you. You must deny him that time by turning him off with gunfire. That means hitting him. It is nearly impossible to hit a target accurately while on the run. Extend the distance and it gets even more difficult. Shots may be fired, yes, but any hits will be more a matter of luck than design. When close to the adversary, you must hit him, stop his actions, and then get behind cover.

Examine your immediate environment and determine what objects would constitute good cover and also just good concealment. Keep in mind the types of weapons that are likely to be in the hands of attackers. Automobiles, for example, make relatively good cover against buckshot and pistol ammunition but not against centerfire rifle ammunition or some exotic shotgun slugs. The exception here would be side window glass that is easily penetrated by the most puny of rounds.

Some types of cover may actually cause bullets to ricochet. Bullets will tend to ricochet on a path approximately parallel to, and a few inches out from, the surface that they've hit. This means that your adversary's bullet may travel along the surface of your cover right into you! You must maintain a safe distance of about 6 feet from the item used for cover.

You may or may not know the ballistic capability of your adversary's weapon nor the effect that it may have on your chosen cover. Rather than being disappointed in your cover's performance, seek as solid a protection as possible, given the time and distance allowed. This way even if he's armed with a rifle you'll have it covered.

When you are shooting from behind cover, don't expose any more of yourself to gunfire than is necessary to shoot back. There are various shooting positions that will allow the maximum use of cover by conforming to its characteristics. Learn them!

When you emerge from cover to shoot, use the least amount of movement possible. Allow the muzzle to precede your eye in a firing position, shoot, and withdraw the way you came. Do not let the muzzle protrude beyond cover at any time—remember to keep back from the cover. Avoid physically taxing positions or shooting from the support side.

Anticipation of danger is a product of awareness. Awareness comes from a proper mind-set and attitude. In earlier times, the penalty for a sentry who had been surprised was death. Similarly, for police or private citizens, being taken unaware will decrease their survival potential considerably. The idea is to know that there is going to be a fight before it starts. If you are prepared for it, you can dictate the course of the fight as it unfolds and keep all your bases . . . well . . . "covered."

Wounded Shooter Techniques

My old martial arts teacher used to say that you should not begin a fight without expecting to get hurt. A corollary of that wisdom would be that you should not dismiss the possibility of being shot in a gunfight. This point is further driven home when you remember that you must often allow the other guy to make the first move. Your conditions of readiness to the contrary, you might even get shot without warning or opportunity to produce your own pistol. You may not even know where your adversary is!

If you are hit with gunfire unexpectedly, your first concern should be to seek cover as soon as it is tactically possible. Seeking cover is primary in situations where the source of the gunfire is not known (if you don't know the source of the attack you can't counterattack). Clearly if an immediate counterattack is possible, it is preferred. When your adversary realizes that his gunfire has been effective, he'll probably decide to move in for the kill. Your ability to shoot him before he can shoot you again will determine whether you live or die.

I have never been shot, but I've spoken with men on both sides of the law who have been shot, as well as having witnessed several shootings firsthand. Reactions to gunshot wounds seem to depend on two things. The first is the state of mind of the victim prior to being shot as well as what he "expected" to happen when he was shot. This determines

The ability to execute a draw and shoot with a single hand is important in the event that the other hand is wounded.

psychological reaction, if any. The second is the actual damage caused by the bullet.

The psychological reaction may be affected by involuntary physical shock resulting from internal injury. The psychological reaction will also determine your reactions if the wound is not of a serious or life-threatening nature. Your ability to function will depend on where you are hit and how bad. Some people don't even realize that they've been shot until later, even though their wounds are serious. Other people will fall down and die from inconsequential wounds. The bottom line is that if you can still think and move (albeit in a limited capacity), you can still fight.

It is important to learn how to manage your pistol with either hand in the event that the other one is disabled by gunfire. This includes not only drawing and shooting but also reloading and clearing malfunctions. Keep in mind that your support hand's trigger finger will not be as "educated" as your strong trigger finger, so it is imperative to keep it clear of the trigger during nonshooting activities.

The strong-hand-only draw is the same as the standard draw exclusive of the support hand. The support-hand-only draw involves reaching behind the back to the holstered pistol and obtaining a full grip around the butt. Bring the pistol out and around to the front, regripping as needed on the way up to the target. If the behind-the-back draw is not functional because of physical limitations or holster position, you must reach across the front, draw upside down and, using "body English," hold the pistol against your body while you regrip it properly and move it toward the target.

To reload the pistol using the strong hand only, eject the magazine and place the pistol barrel down between your knees. Holding the pistol in place with inward pressure from the knees, retrieve a fresh magazine one-handed and insert it

Reloading the pistol one-handed is another useful skill. First, eject the spent magazine.

Place the pistol between the knees and hold it there.

Retrieve a fresh magazine.

Insert it into the pistol.

Seat the magazine fully in the magazine well.

Regrip the pistol and get back on target.

into the pistol. Regrip the pistol in a firing grip, activate the slide release lever to chamber a cartridge, and bring it back on target.

A support-hand-only reload is similar. Depress the magazine button with the trigger finger and proceed as before with the appropriate hand.

Needing to clear a pistol malfunction one handed after you've just been shot will not be a very cheerful experience, but with a little forethought you'll be able to handle it quickly and efficiently. Basically, you need to locate any projection on the pistol slide that you can use to catch onto a belt, holster, or other handy piece of gear in order to actuate the slide. The rear sight of most pistols will serve perfectly. Some pistols, such as the Smith & Wesson autoloading pistols equipped with the Novak sight, do not have usable projections on the sights. With these you must use the ejection port itself or the ubiquitous slide-mounted decocking lever. If all else fails, you can use the front sight to press against a solid object (not your belt or holster in this case, please) to actuate the slide.

For the position one malfunction (failure to fire), strike the floorplate of the magazine against your hip or knee and actuate the slide by hooking the rear sight (or other slide projection) on your belt or holster. This same series of moves will also clear a position two malfunction (failure to eject).

Clearing a malfunction while wounded will not be a very enjoyable event, but it can be done with a little preplanning. Here we see a position two malfunction (stovepipe).

The situation becomes worrisome indeed if you need to clear a position three malfunction (feedway stoppage) one-handed after being wounded. If you are in possession of a back-up pistol, this would be a good time to bring it into action.

To clear a P-3 with the strong hand, lock the slide to the rear by using the thumb to activate the slide lock lever as you hook the rear sight (or other slide projection) on your holster and pull the slide back. Eject the existing magazine and release the slide, allowing it to go forward. Using the same slide projection, actuate the slide back and forth several times to clear the feed ramp area. Next, place the pistol between your knees as in the reloading drill and reload a

TAP the magazine bottom on the knee.

HOOK the offending cartridge case (or other projection on the pistol slide) onto the holster (or off-side magazine pouch).

Use it to RACK the slide, thereby ejecting the offending case and chambering a fresh round.

Back on target.

Clearing a position three malfunction one-handed (and under fire?) is quite a chore.

A viable option is to discard the inoperative pistol and . . .

. . . retrieve your back-up pistol to solve the problem!

fresh magazine into the pistol. A final actuation of the pistol slide chambers a fresh cartridge, and you are back in the fight. The execution for the support hand is identical except that you use the trigger finger instead of the thumb.

All of these one-handed methods should be practiced standing, seated, and on your knees. Considering the possibility that you may actually be knocked off your feet, practice on your back as well.

Shooting back when you've been knocked down is a different issue completely. Since cover is one primary concern, your position must conform to that cover if possible. If you are knocked down, you are better able to return fire if you can roll over onto your back rather than remain face down. Shooting from a supine position (face up) generally requires less physical strength, which is an important issue for someone who's just been shot. All a supine shooter needs to do is raise the head slightly and look at the target. A prone shooter must almost raise his entire upper body off the deck to see or shoot. Remember, these are going to be situations where the adversary is in close proximity.

Returning fire to a close-range target one-handed from a prone position is problematic.

A more efficient way is to take a supine position, facilitating one-handed shooting to just about all angles.

The most effective method of returning fire from the ground is a variation of the silhouette shooting position. Simply place the shooting hand(s) between the knees and bring the knees together for support. Holding the pistol in this position, you are ready to shoot. This position is predicated on being able to contract the stomach muscles to enable you to lift your upper body slightly. If you cannot do this, you must shoot one-handed at the adversary in whichever direction he attacks from.

The great World War II German ace Hans-Ulrich Rudel said, "A man is only beaten when he admits it to himself." Such an attitude—and a little luck—will see you through if you ever need to resort to wounded shooter techniques.

One Against Many: Dealing with Multiple Adversaries

Predatory criminals like to stack the odds in their favor. Particularly, criminals are likely to join in a group to commit their assaults. Looking back at Chapter 4 on the dynamics of gunfights, you can see that there is a very real probability of having to face more than one adversary.

When the targets multiply, so does your exposure to danger. Ideally, your alert attitude and combat mind-set will provide prior warning to the situation that is unfolding before you. If that happens, a tactical withdrawal would be wise before the shooting starts. If not an escape, such a tactical withdrawal might lead you to a position of cover from which you might mount an unexpected counterattack of your own when they don't expect it. In any case, waiting until they are on top of you before reacting is foolish if you have prior warning.

More likely, a situation involving multiple adversaries will be one where you've surprised *them* in the middle of some sort of crime. Your response in such a case will be dependent on your awareness, readiness to act, and particular interest in the situation. For example, if you see three armed and masked men as you stroll past an open business, your response will be different than if you encounter the same three men in your living room at 0'dark 30!

During the preconfrontation period, if withdrawing is not an option, you must begin looking for things to use as cover. Ideally, your chosen position will place you on an enfilade— that is, you will be able to fire into them along a linear axis rather than across their line abreast.

If shooting is the option, fire first at the man whose attention

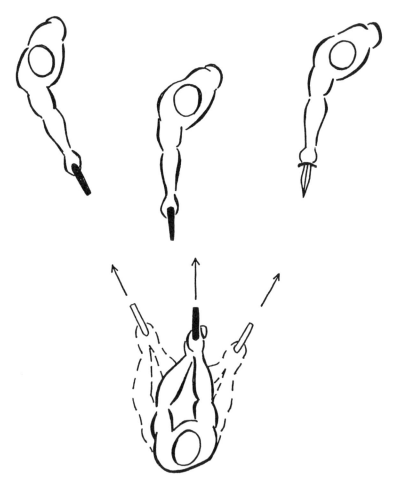

Facing three adversaries standing abreast is a bad situation. They can all shoot you simultaneously, whereas you can only shoot at each one individually.

is most focused toward you. This does not necessarily mean the one with the most powerful weapon. Shoot the man most immediately capable of killing you in your present position.

Get behind cover as soon as the situation allows. If you

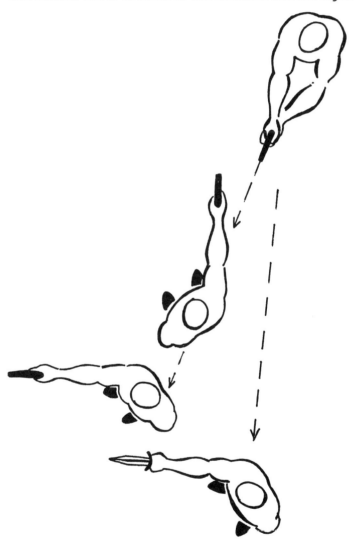

A better situation is to engage them when they are more or less standing in line so that you can place effective fire on all of them simultaneously while they cannot do the same to you.

are already under fire, you must deal with the situation in an aggressive manner before moving to cover, or, better yet, shoot on the move as you travel to cover.

If the cover shields you from only some of the adversaries, shoot those whom you are still exposed to first. There is no place for discussions or negotiations here. Once the fight has begun, you'd better keep shooting until they are all down or until you can extract out of there.

You must develop the ability to "roll out" from behind cover in a shooting position behind your gun muzzle without overexposing yourself to incoming fire.

When dealing with single opponents, you can afford to "hammer" them into submission if that is necessary. You do not have that option when facing a group. Other than to shoot the most immediate threat first, it is vital to get a hit on each man once and to do it quickly. Shoot each man once and move on to the next one, picking up any remaining targets afterward. Engage the targets alternately until they are all down. Do not pummel one particular man with an entire magazine and ignore the others. You must evaluate as you shoot—that is, let the eyes come off the sights and travel downrange to "evaluate" the results after you've swept them once. The pistol remains pointed at the adversaries in a firing position if more shots are needed.

You want to sweep across the group from strong side to weak side. Looking back at Chapter 13 on close-quarters combat, we discussed how much easier it is to track, with the gun muzzle, a target that is toward the "inside" of the gun hand. Conversely, it is more difficult to do so with a target on the "outside" of that hand. Shooting from strong side to weak side is physically more efficient than the reverse since it follows the natural range of movement of the body. This does not preclude dealing with the immediate threat first, which may determine the path of your gun muzzle. The final word is to be able to shoot both ways, but just realize that one way is faster.

Ammunition depletion is a real concern when facing multiple opponents, so an extra magazine (or two) is a good idea. Firepower is not a solution to tactical problems, but it is comforting to have a few extra rounds just in case.

The act of shooting two, three, or even four targets in a short time frame is not physically difficult. There is an interval between shots fired that competition shooters call "dwell time." Dwell time occurs between the point when the first shot is actually fired and the point when the pistol is realigned on target after the recoil cycle. This dwell time varies between 1/4 and 1/2 second, depending on the shooter's ability. Use this time to "travel" or move the pistol from one target to the next. Move the muzzle toward the next target on the recoil so that when you reacquire the sights, you will already be aligned on the next target.

The eyes will be involved to a great degree in picking up flash sight pictures and in glancing downrange to check if the targets are still standing. Targets very close together abreast or staggered can be shot very quickly. Visually pick up the first target and align the pistol on it. As the shot is fired, the visual focus remains on the front sight as the pistol travels to the next target during recoil. When you notice that you have arrived at the next target in your peripheral vision, fire the shot.

If the targets are spread out, the problem is more difficult. You must still visually acquire the first target and shoot it in the same way. Now as the pistol rises in recoil and travels toward where you believe the next target is, the visual focus leaves the pistol sights and precedes the pistol to that target. When the pistol catches up to the eye, the eye looks for whatever sort of sight picture is required to make the shot and the shot is fired.

There is no easy answer to the multiple target problem. This is a very difficult tactical situation that you would not choose to face purposely. The best course of action is to withdraw. If they follow, pick them off one by one guerrilla-style during a tactical retreat. If you have a reasonable belief that those armed men are there for you and escape is not a likely option, you'd best place *them* on the defensive and attack immediately. You do not need to be under fire before acting. Being alert to your surroundings is the best option of all, because if you see trouble coming, you can prepare for it. For example, if you suddenly look up from your newspaper at the local coffeehouse and see T-Bone with his two young inner-city associates facing you with sawed-off shotguns, you've probably already lost that fight. On the other hand, if you see the same trio prying open your kitchen window and entering your home on a quiet summer night, *you've* won that fight.

Operating in Reduced-Light Environments

Criminals, like most predators, favor the dark. Is it any surprise then that most pistol fights occur at night or in dim light? This fact alone has given rise to an entire industry devoted to solving the plight of the night fighter.

Most of the products aimed at this problem are, unfortunately, useless gadgets. Other products available may work in some environments but not in others. Of those that are useful, each one has certain advantages and shortcomings. It is incumbent upon you to choose your gear wisely based on your real world needs.

The problem in reduced-light environments is not to identify the sights but rather to locate and identify the target. Let's analyze the different light scenarios to illustrate the problem.

You are generally not going to operate in complete darkness. Unless you are "hunting" an adversary in a darkened and windowless warehouse, there will be some degree of ambient light available. While increments of light and dark do not fall into neat categories, we have nonetheless categorized them into four levels to demonstrate the peculiarities of varying light levels.

The first light level is dusk. This level lasts from just before sunset to about a half hour after sunset. The available light still allows you to easily distinguish your surroundings and people present in the area. You can still see the sights on your pistol, albeit not as clearly as at high noon. Shooting is no different than at any other time. Target identification is not a problem.

About a half hour after sunset you will find yourself at the second level in semidarkness. You can still see your surroundings and distinguish persons in the area, but they are now back-lit or silhouetted by the fading light still visible in the sky. You can no longer see your sights easily. The now black sights tend to disappear when they are superimposed on a silhouetted target. You know where the sights are, and you can still verify a "rough" sight picture, but your reliance on programmed muscle-memory to index the pistol on target is considerably greater. Anything beyond close-range shooting is very difficult. This is where radioactive night sights shine (excuse the pun). When you bring a pistol so equipped on target, you see the glowing elements of the sights instead of black blurry sights on a black fuzzy target.

As the level of ambient light decreases further, you will find that it becomes increasingly difficult to locate and identify targets. You can still see your surroundings, but persons in the area are seen as indistinct shadows that seemingly melt into the dark background. You cannot see your sights at all. To operate in this level of light, you need some sort of flashlight to locate and identify possible targets. A flashlight will work well at this level as well as at the previous, brighter level. Night sights will not work here because they are not used for locating or identifying targets. When you illuminate a target with a flashlight, your sights (tritium equipped or not) will appear as black sights silhouetted on the light background that is the illuminated target. If you use the tritium-equipped sight without the aid of a flashlight, you will not know that there is even a target there!

Any further decrease in ambient light places you in the realm of complete darkness. Here you can see absolutely nothing. Since there is no light, there is no visual input to indicate anything at all. You do, however, still have audio input in the form of sounds. You cannot see the target, but you might be able to hear where he is. You can listen for breathing, footsteps, or any sound that might be man-made. These sounds are target indicators that tell you that someone is nearby. By listening for these target indicators, you can index your light and gun to the source of that sound.

It is reflexive to turn and look in the direction of a sound. You train to coordinate your gun muzzle with the direction of your visual focus, don't you? Eyes, muzzle, and target in line! Everything remains the same except that you do not have a target. You do, however, have a sound that might indicate that target. So you think, "eyes, muzzle, sound (and possibly target) in line!" This is the "three eye" principle at its best—the pistol muzzle is the third eye and it "looks" in the same direction as the other two eyes. If you "lock in" on the sound, you may "lock in" on the target. Since there is no light you still have to illuminate the source of the sound and possibly the person who made it to determine whether he is friend or foe.

As comical as it may sound, don't dismiss olfactory target indicators as well. Criminals are not famous for their personal hygiene, and you might actually be able to smell them hiding in a darkened room without needing a light at all!

These light levels are only generalizations to illustrate problems that vary with the amount of light present. Any state of darkness can be mitigated by varying degrees of ambient light, particularly in urban settings where one might go from high noon to darkness by simply entering a building.

Obviously if there is enough ambient light to see and identify both target and sights, any shooting aids are inconsequential. If there is not enough light to see the sights clearly but the targets are visible as backlit shadows, you can use either night sights (if you are certain that the targets are hostile without illuminating them) or a flashlight to light them up in order to determine their status. When the background blends with possible targets, flashlights become mandatory and other sight enhancements are moot. Clearly a flashlight is the more versatile of all accessories for night shooting. Realize, however, that the flashlight is not intended as an aid to sight the shots but rather only as a means to locate and identify targets.

An option that many tech junkies tout as the wave of the future is the laser sight. Lasers have some utility in infrared configurations that are invisible to the human eye and are intended for operators wearing night vision goggles. Such systems provide true night fighting capability without sacrificing any stealth. Unfortunately, they are expensive enough to be beyond consideration . . . unless the taxpayers are signing the check (and who goes around with a set of night vision goggles strapped to his head all the time anyway?).

Other over-the-counter laser sights are really a solution in search of a problem. They do nothing to help locate or identify targets, nor do they illuminate existing sighting systems. Users develop the bad habit of looking downrange to "find" the dot and "move" it onto the target. This costs precious time that you just do not have. If you are working in conjunction with other operators (read that, tactical team), how will you be able to distinguish your dot from the others when more than one team member "beams" a target? Laser sights are fine in the specialized infrared format; visible light, over-the-counter laser sights are neat toys and nothing more.

There are three methods for incorporating a flashlight and a pistol. All three will work, so pay your money and take your choice. The important thing here is to be able to establish coaxality between the light beam and the axis of the gun barrel. You don't just want to locate and identify a potential hostile; you want to be able to shoot him the instant a threat is realized. Of the plethora of flashlight methods, there are three that best fulfill your tactical needs. Remember that you do not "speed draw" into a flashlight position. If you perceive an immediate threat, handle it without resorting to the flashlight. If there is enough light to recognize the threat, there is enough light to handle it using standard means. Otherwise you wouldn't have seen it in the first place. There will always be ample time to realize you are entering a reduced-light environment and to make a point of securing a flashlight.

The best option for dealing with the problems of a low-light environment is a weapon-mounted flashlight such as this Laser Products Sure-Fire tactical light.

The first way to incorporate a light with a pistol is simply to bolt one on. My SWAT pistol has a Sure-Fire light module attached under the receiver. Equipping a pistol thus can be done for a couple of C-notes. The special ops style scenario sometimes requires a free hand, which makes carrying or holding a separate light a somewhat clumsy act. A bolted-on light unit frees that hand for when it is needed. Additionally, a light-equipped pistol does not require learning a "new" and different shooting technique. You simply shoot with both hands on the pistol as you normally do. You are never without a light whenever you have your pistol with you, and that light is bright enough for any realistic tactical need. While such a pistol is not a first choice to stuff into a concealment holster on a summer day, it is a viable system for uniformed officers and home defenders as well as SWAT officers.

A second way to coordinate gun with light was devel-

The Harries flashlight position.

oped by former Gunsite instructor Mike Harries. This method is, of course, called the Harries method. It is the most rigid and accurate of the flashlight techniques.

The flashlight is held in the "clubbing" position with the lens at the bottom of the fist. The drawn pistol is held out by the strong hand in a one-handed low ready hold. The flashlight hand is brought underneath the drawn pistol and back against the strong hand. In effect, back of left hand meets back of right hand and a slight counterpressure is exerted which will function to dampen muzzle flip. If you are using a long five- or six-cell Maglite type flashlight, it is helpful to index the endcap of the light against the strong-side forearm. The light switch can be operated by any of the fingers of the support hand, or, in the case of the Sure-Fire lights with their endcap buttons, the support-side thumb. (Incidentally, all tactical-type flashlights must have momentary on-off switches.) The flashlight also is suitably positioned for use as a contact weapon if alternate force is called for.

The third flashlight technique was developed by Ray Chapman. Here the flashlight is again held by the support hand, specifically by the thumb and index fingers in a sort of OK sign. The remaining three fingers are wrapped around the pistol in the standard manner. The light switch is actuated by either the thumb or index finger of the support hand. It is not as rigid as the Harries but is considerably easier for those with shoulder injuries. Additionally, it deviates less from the standard shooting position than the Harries.

When using a flashlight in a tactical scenario, do not light up and stroll through the woods. Avoid lighting up the scene until you absolutely need to do so. You know that noise is a target indicator—well, so is light! A beam of light moving In the criminal's direction tells him that someone is looking for him. Be frugal with the light! Be careful with the finger pres-

The Chapman flashlight technique.

sure on the light switch too. The last thing you want when searching for an armed criminal is a white light A.D. (a momentary unintentional turning on of a flashlight), which advises those for whom you are searching that you are in the area and what your intentions are. Such a thing will give you away as surely as if you'd shot a round into the floor!

Let's examine the situations where tactical flashlight use will likely be needed. Using a flashlight in conjunction with a pistol is a conscious pro-active decision, not a reactive one. You will have some indication for the need to secure a light to solve a tactical problem. You are, in essence, using the pistol and the light in an offensive role, not a defensive one. You are not reacting to a target but rather you are seeking a target. This is evident even in a defensive home scenario where the resident ensconces himself and waits for the intruder to come to

The Sure-Fire flashlight technique.

The Harries technique with a Sure-Fire flashlight.

him. The resident, hidden from the criminal, will initiate the action by illuminating and possibly shooting the intruder.

Police officers are often tasked with conducting building searches ranging from simple alarm checks to full-bore tactical entries. Dynamic/explosive clearing aside, you often have the element of surprise on your side. If it is available, you are well advised to scan any area to be searched from behind cover. Move to cover with stealth and light up the area for no more than two seconds as you scan for hostiles, ready to shoot. Flick off the light, move to the next vantage point, and repeat as needed. Unless you are involved in a hostage rescue, time is on your side and you needn't rush.

When scanning a room, remain low and beam the light upward into the ceiling. The light will "bounce" off the ceiling and wash the entire room with enough light to see what is within. If you are working with a partner, he can light up the room in this manner as you move forward and search under and outside the beam of light. You will be virtually invisible to anyone at whom the light is pointed. If the light is actually pointing at the criminal's hiding place, he will need to decide whether he wants to fight or stay hidden. If he chooses to fight the man with the light, shoot him. Problem solved. If he remains hidden, he will likely remain so while the light is covering his position. This allows you to approach in stealth and deal with him from a position of advantage. If you get the idea that searching in the dark is not a wise solitary pastime, you are quite right!

If you cannot locate cover from which to launch your search, you are truly at a disadvantage. In this case, you must move, light and scan, and move again, being as quiet and stealthy as you can. Avoid presenting yourself as a stationary lit-up target! Understand also that as soon as your light goes on, your night vision is history and it will not return fully for several minutes.

Solving tactical problems in reduced light is difficult, but it is a fact of life. These ideas and techniques will help shed some light on the matter when you go in search of things that go bump in the night!

Tactical Movement

Gunfights are not stationary and static affairs; they are moving and dynamic. At advanced levels it is important to develop and cultivate the ability to shoot on the move. By shooting on the move I mean substantially more movement than the emergency sidestep or backstep used in arm's-reach encounters. Do not confuse this with the notion of shooting during a full sprint. I once had to shoot during a dead run, and I do not recommend it.

You might need to shoot while moving to cover, while changing to a different covered location, or even while evacuating a location. You could also be trying to move quickly through an area containing multiple possible adversaries or conducting a semihurried search, or you might be involved in a tactical team scenario conducting a dynamic entry. In these circumstances, it is important to not lose momentum, particularly in the tactical team scenario. If you lose momentum here, the others behind you trying to reach the same objective will be affected. If you stop suddenly, the entire team will be bottlenecked, with potentially fatal results. The ability to shoot and approach the target also has an over-

Shooting on the move involves keeping the front sight (and subsequently the muzzle) steady while walking.

whelming effect that may give you the necessary edge to win. Whatever the reason, shooting on the move is a useful skill to have in the tactical bag of tricks.

The main thing to remember when moving is to alter the style of shooting as little as possible. The upper body from the waist up is the gun mount. The legs are the shock absorbers and transportation. Move with the gun mounted in a ready-to-shoot position with the muzzle lowered just enough to be able to see downrange but not quite pointing at the floor. The waist must be able to turn left or right in order to cover danger areas on the move. When actually moving, simply walk normally as you would during everyday transportation. The only differences are that the knees are bent slightly, lowering the body, there is a slight forward lean evident, and the walk involves a rolling heel-toe stride. Moving forward or backward is possible with this type of walk.

Whether moving forward or backing up, it is important to remember not to walk faster than you can shoot. This usually means a brisk walking pace (neither a leisurely stroll nor a full run). Practice by placing a quarter on the top of the pistol's slide and walking forward and backward several times, experimenting with the speed. The object of the drill is to minimize any up and down bobbing of the front sight and muzzle. Walk only as fast as you can while keeping the coin from falling off the slide. The eyes are downrange, searching, looking, and hunting for targets. As soon as a target is located, the sights interrupt the eye/target line and any necessary shots are fired.

To practice tactical movement, you need a range that is about 25 yards long with pairs of paper humanoid targets every 5 yards. There must be enough space between the targets to allow you to walk comfortably between them. And that is exactly what you will do. Move forward, engaging the targets with two shots apiece right and left. As this becomes easier, some of the targets can be replaced with barricades or positions of cover that you can move to and emerge from as you engage the targets on the move.

The same exercise can be used in reverse (walking backward), engaging the same targets as you withdraw from the scene. As you come abreast of the next set of targets, shoot the targets in front of you when you reach the 5 yard line. The walk here is the same except that you really have to be sensitive to where your feet are stepping. The same rolling gait is used except that you step back with the toes first and then roll backward onto the heel, actually feeling your way back as you step. The drill is a training exercise designed to provide fresh targets every few steps. If there really were ten hostiles behind you, you would not back up toward them!

Shooting on a parallel or diagonal line is a different situation requiring a certain amount of flexibility in the rotation of the waist. The method of approach is the same, but the targets will appear parallel to the line of travel. You do not need to be facing them to respond. The feet keep moving in the original direction. The upper torso pivots at the waist toward the target, bringing the pistol in line with the target. Immediately it becomes noticeable that it is substantially easier to engage targets that appear to the support side than those that appear to the strong side. The solution is to "cut" the angle as much as possible or to come in on a diagonal line. Targets on the support side can be engaged at a 90 degree angle or greater, whereas targets on the strong side cannot be engaged at more than about 60 degrees.

If while moving along the "firing line" a target appears 90 degrees to the strong side, extend the left arm as you rotate the waist and gun mount toward the target and tran-

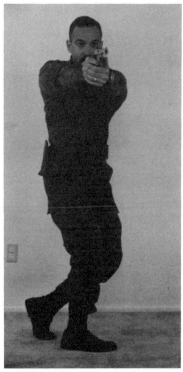

Engaging a threat to the support side on the move involves simply pivoting at the waist and shooting.

Engaging a threat to the strong side on the move may require a momentary shift into the isosceles position in order to facilitate torso rotation.

sition from the Weaver to a momentary isosceles shooting position. The other alternative (particularly if long guns are used) is to turn mid-stride to the strong side to engage. You will actually be shooting while backing up. This is accomplished by stepping forward and across the line of travel with the support side foot and simultaneously bringing the strong side foot around and back. After the shot is fired, it is a simple matter to pivot back around, resuming the forward movement.

Practice this by setting up five targets along a straight line about 5 yards downrange parallel to the line of travel and 3 yards apart edge to edge. With the targets to the right or left, begin walking, engaging the targets as you walk past them from 45 to 90 degree angles. Avoid shooting until the targets are about 5 yards away. Shooting at too great an angle or at too distant a target is not the object of the drill. The drill can be executed forward as well as backward.

Practice these drills: forward, backward, parallel targets to the right, and parallel targets to the left. Execute them slowly at first and with dry firing. Add the 25 cent element to eliminate any up and down bobbing action in the walk. Walk normally except for the slight forward lean, slightly bent knees, and rolling gait. No exaggerated walk here—Groucho was a comedian, not a tactics instructor!

During stealth searches, certain tactical obstacles will need to be secured and negotiated. Unless you are involved in a dynamic entry or under fire, you will want to move with stealth. The same movement drill applies, but it now becomes substantially slower and more deliberate.

When nearing a geographic threat that is likely to contain an enemy, things slow down even more. The walk now becomes a shuffle step for approaching the last few feet toward a danger area and a possible con-

Do not violate the "three eye principle" and visually look at a possible threat without also "looking" at it (covering it) with the muzzle.

If you turn to look at something, do so with the entire shooting platform.

When approaching a threat area where contact with the adversary is likely, the shuffle step developed by Chuck Taylor is the best option.

frontation. This is the same footwork used when "cutting the pie" on a doorway or negotiating a corner. It involves taking a half-step forward with the forward foot and catching up with a half-step forward with the back foot. The feet do not drag or scrape on the deck. Some police trainers have called this the "stomp-drag" method. It is neither a stomp nor a drag. The step is most similar to the way you would walk while trying to pass sideways through a particularly narrow hallway that cannot accommodate the width of the hips. The advantage of this shuffle step is that it offers very controlled movement and enables the shooter to respond from a very stable position even if caught mid-stride.

You might be already on the move simply walking

Response to a threat at the strong side.

Pivot on the toes toward the threat and grip the holstered pistol.

somewhere when a threat appears at any point on 360 degrees. It is better to draw and shoot mid-stride than to suddenly stop in your tracks. If a threat pops up in your path, attack and overwhelm it instead of stopping and backpedaling. Even better, move laterally on the draw first and then approach forward.

If the threat appears to either side, the response is slightly different. You can respond from a stationary point without moving more than an initial step, or you can respond from a walk without breaking stride.

Let's examine the response to a target on the right side. Realizing a threat to the right, pivot on the toe of the left foot and on the heel of the right foot. Now push off the left foot

and step forward toward the target. The draw is simultaneous with the footwork. In response to the right from a moving position, simply step forward with the foot that is away from the target, pivoting as you step—in this case, with the left foot. You now push off the left foot as you draw and step toward the target with the right (strong-side) foot.

Responding to the left is similar. Step forward with the foot that is away from the target—in this case the right foot—and pivot on the right toes toward the target. From a forward walk the

Step forward and bring the pistol on target.

Response to a threat at the support side.

Step forward with the strong-side foot and grip the pistol.

motion is identical. Pivot on the right foot as you step and continue the walk with the left foot toward the target as you draw.

Responding to a threat behind you requires a 180 degree pivot. Facing away from the target, step forward and across with the right foot as the hand moves to the pistol. Then pivot on the right foot and face the target as you complete the draw. If you are walking away, the drill is the same. Step forward during the draw and pivot toward the target as before.

The rule of thumb is to pivot on the foot that is away

Pivot toward the threat . . .   *. . . and bring the pistol on target.*

from the target. The hand moves toward the pistol the instant the threat is realized, and the pistol is brought on target as the footwork is completed. The forward motion can either be arrested, initiated, or continued depending on the tactical need. The pivots should be identical whether you are on the move or stationary. These responses can also be turned in to supported positions such as kneeling or prone or made into lateral movements to cover. The possibilities are endless.

Rarely will an adversary plant his feet and stand facing you ready for the showdown like the targets at the range. Even if

Response to a threat from the rear.   *Step across the centerline and grip the pistol.*

he did, you should be moving as you shoot to avoid being hit yourself. Attackers, especially predatory criminals, prefer sneaking up on their victims. They won't let you know that they are coming. The FBI statistics on police officers killed in gunfights tells us that when interviewed, many of the cop killers said they took the officer by surprise and there was nothing he could have done to prevent it. Part of the solution is clearly that of mind-set, but the second part is to be able to respond to any point on a 360 degree circle. These tactical movement drills will help you do exactly that when you find it necessary to think on your feet.

*Pivot toward the threat and bring
the pistol on target.*

Seated responses are important to practice, but care must be exercised on the draw to avoid "sweeping" your legs with the muzzle.

Grip the pistol.

Pivot toward the threat and bring the pistol on target.

Threat to the support side. Grip the pistol . . .

. . . and pivot to get on target. Be careful not to sweep your legs on the draw.

Threat from the rear. Grip the pistol and begin to turn to the support side.

Pivot to face the threat and get the pistol on target.

Sometimes you may not be able to get up from your chair and will need to solve the problem seated.

Indoor Search Tactics

It is a myth that a single individual can safely and success-fully search and clear an entire house single-handedly. This myth is easily "shot down" if you think of a building search as negotiating a series of geographic threats. A geographic threat is any structure, item, or architectural feature that might contain a physical threat (a bad guy). It is simply impossible for one person to cover and control two separate geographic threats in two different directions. When faced with two such geographic threats, the operator must eventu-ally turn his back on one in order to check the other. This is a violation of sound tactical principles, and survival will depend more on good luck than good tactics. Even those who conduct building searches regularly send at least two, sometimes three men to clear one room.

The principles of MOUT (military operations in urban ter-rain) teach us that built-up areas (such as a house) over-whelmingly favor the defender. The greatest danger to a searcher is the ability of an adversary to hide and simply lie in wait for the searcher. This can be used to great advantage by the homeowner by simply waiting for the bad guy to come to him. A good plan would be first to secure loved ones in a safe room, call for reinforcements (i.e. the police), and wait armed, ready, and behind cover for the aggressor to come.

The problem is that sometimes you won't be sure enough to call the police when that strange noise rouses you out of a sound sleep. Additionally, what if that sound of glass breaking came from a loved one's room way across the house? You will all probably go see for yourself, and it is with that understanding that you proceed with an examination of building searches.

A homeowner's objectives are to secure and protect immediate family members and to establish if in fact an invasion has occurred. Under such circumstances, you must move as fast as tactically possible to secure and relocate family members. If you choose to proceed with the search at this point, stealth must be foremost on your mind. Consider also that if you've just been awakened from a sound sleep, it will take a few moments to shake out those mental cobwebs before proceeding.

While there are no standard buildings, there are standard moves and concepts that will suit all types of buildings. The first consideration is to use all of your senses (sight, hearing, smell, and touch) to seek out target indicators. A target indicator is any tell-tale sign that the adversary is nearby or present. Such indicators can vary from hearing a footfall to seeing the brim of a hat protruding from a doorway or even smelling an unwashed adversary's body odor.

I remember one search where a suspect ran away from us toward the back room of a house. After securing the immediate scene, we conducted a painfully slow and thorough search of the remainder of the house. During a search of the room we believed the suspect to be hiding in, I reached out to open a cabinet. It was a very cold day, and as

I touched the door of the cabinet to open it, I felt the suspect's body heat radiating through the door crack. We moved our people back, ordered the suspect out, and arrested him without incident.

The lesson here is to be receptive to even the most seemingly inconsequential thing, as it might be a target indicator. You must also take advantage of all your surroundings. This includes picking up reflections from polished surfaces and looking through cracks before opening doors. A second consideration is never to turn your back on anything you've not checked. You cannot assume that a particular room, closet, or whatever is clear until you have physically looked in there and seen all four walls, corners, and the ceiling. You must look into less obvious areas as well. You cannot shoot what you don't realize is there, but what you don't see can certainly shoot you! Additionally, people can hide in the most unexpected places. For example, I would not have thought that the cabinet in our story could have concealed a full-grown man, but it did.

When searching in close quarters, keep the ready position in close to prevent gun grabs as well as to avoid telegraphing your location to the adversary.

The technique of "slicing the pie" on a corner allows the searcher to clear the way incrementally without exposing himself.

You must handle all geographic threats in a tactical manner. When you move, keep your pistol in a ready position and lead with the gun muzzle without letting it precede your entry and protrude into uncleared areas. Be careful to keep your balance and stay in control at all times. Observe the "three eye principle"—that is, two eyes and one gun muzzle. Your eyes and gun muzzle must always be "looking" in the same direction. Any tactical movement, in fact, is simply a way to move your eyes and gun muzzle toward a possible threat and to keep it there while you clear it.

Stay away from corners and any other feature that may contain a physical threat. Clear such features incrementally like cutting a pie. When you cut a pie, you do so one slice at a time. Incremental clearing works the same way. As you approach a corner, look past the corner deeply on an angle. If you do not see any target indicators, move laterally in small increments (staying well back from the corner itself) until you can see that the area beyond the corner is clear of any hostiles.

This is what the searcher sees initially.

One half step later, he sees the hand and the gun. What does that tell him about the individual around the corner and his intentions?

A doorway is handled the same way from one side. If the door is closed, determine which way it opens. Generally, if you can see the hinges, the door opens outward. If you cannot see the hinges, it opens inward. Take a position on either side of the door to allow maximum visibility into the interior of the room as soon as the door begins to swing open. If it opens outward, stand next to the doorknob. If it opens inward, stand across from the doorknob. Hold the pistol in a close weapon-retention position while opening

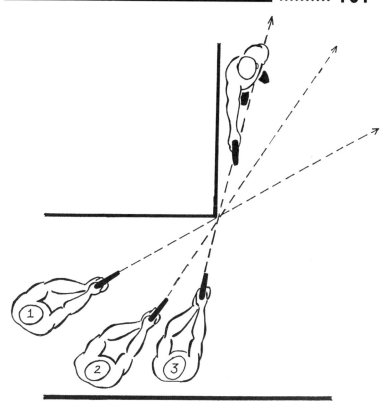

The searcher clears the corner incrementally, eventually observing some portion of the adversary before being seen himself.

the door and keep it there until the door is open and you can extend the pistol to check the room. Do not linger in the doorway because all the adversary needs to do is shoot toward the doorway and possibly hit you. The doorway is called the "fatal funnel," and you must get through it quickly after you've visually checked the interior of the room from the outside.

Visually, search on a vertical axis, moving your search laterally every few feet. Searching vertically (north to south

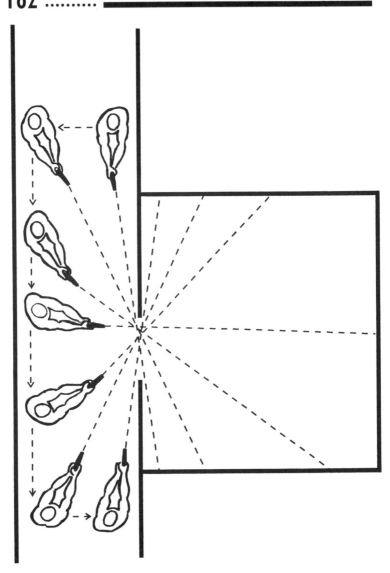

Clearing a room from the outside can be accomplished with the incremental clearing method as well. The searcher's line of sight (and fire) is illustrated with the dotted line.

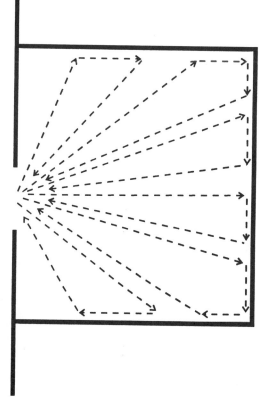

When visually searching an area, it is more efficient to search with a vertical visual scan, allowing the eyes to look at a particular piece of ground several times and from several angles.

instead of east to west) allows your eyes to recheck areas that you might have previously dismissed as clear. Remember, you only need to see a target indicator, not the entire target. A hat brim, the toe of a shoe, or a piece of clothing may be all you need to see.

Stairs present their own set of problems. There is only one way up or down, and it channels your approach as well as any incoming gunfire. Whether clearing upward or downward best depends greatly on your ability to precede your exposure to any threats with the gun muzzle. A stairwell can be divided into the steps and the upper or lower landing. You can clear the steps visually as you approach the stairwell itself. To clear the landing, approach the now

Avoid clearing buildings alone. Even those who do this on a regular basis always send two or three men to search as a team. Here the author is flanked by his teammates Al Acosta and Mike Hurt.

cleared steps and incrementally "cut the pie" until you've cleared what you can of the upper or lower landing (depending on your direction of attack). Then begin the arduous forward move behind your gun muzzle toward the end of the staircase.

When you are moving on the steps themselves, keep your feet toward the edges of the steps and move upward with your back toward but not touching the wall. Avoid placing both feet on one step, and maintain balance at all times. Now consider that there are often two or three sides to an upper landing. You can only realistically cover one side at one time!

Hallways present linear hazards similar to stairways as well as hazards from doorways that open onto them. When moving down hallways, the need to have your back covered is again illustrated. When you approach any doorway adja-

Shooting houses such as this one are invaluable in developing good searching and clearing tactics.

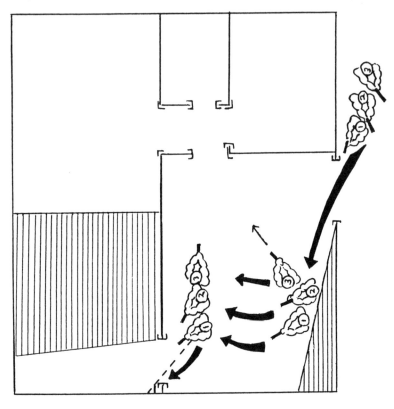

Dynamic entry drills require teamwork and sound tactics.

cent to a hallway, you cannot negotiate the doorway and still keep the hallway covered.

A T-shaped intersection is a hallway that intersects perpendicularly to another hallway. This, in effect, gives you two separate corners opposite from each other. Here you must proceed the same way as if you were clearing a large doorway. You will reach a point where you must again "toss the dice" and clear one corner before the other.

Do not hesitate to stop and simply listen for a while during the search—the adversary will often give himself away with noise. Also, there is no rule preventing you from squatting down or moving on your knees to take advantage of cover or to look through furniture. While moving through open areas, walk briskly but quietly. But when you approach a potential hazard, slow down considerably and use a stealthy shuffle step.

Single-handedly clearing a building is an exercise in luck and not a good idea. Sometimes, however, you cannot avoid such things. At such times, these tactical guidelines will help.

chapter 21

Holding Hostiles at Gunpoint

You've gone to check on that strange noise late one night and found yourself face to face with an intruder in your living room. You've remembered your training and used good tactics while confronting him. You were ready to shoot, but the circumstances did not justify it. You're holding him at gunpoint. Now what?

When holding an adversary at gunpoint in a situation that does not yet allow shooting, there are three consecutive things which need to be done: 1) establish scene dominance (stabilize the situation), 2) disarm the aggressor, and 3) secure the aggressor.

The way to establish scene dominance is to take a position from which to bring effective fire on the target without being exposed to possible incoming fire. This means to *use cover.*

Since you are initiating the confrontation, you're in a position to dictate the circumstances of engagement (as opposed to being surprised and having to counterattack immediately). This means that you can move to a covered position before announcing yourself. It would also be appropriate to approach from behind if possible and to maximize the distance from the danger while still remaining in close enough proximity to handle the situation.

Once you are behind cover and have the muzzle of your weapon covering the target, you can issue the verbal challenge to the hostile. Remember, we are discussing the "no-shoot" situation. If you were in imminent danger you'd simply shoot him. Remember also, there is no guarantee that he will comply with your orders. He may just as easily turn and shoot at the source of the sound. If that occurs, your no-shoot situation has dissolved. You must shoot him before he completes his turn or makes any other movement which will bring his weapon to bear on your position. Even if he initially complies with your wishes, he may have hopes of turning the tables on you, so you must be prepared to deck him if he tries.

The pistol muzzle is pointing at the adversary but is lowered sufficiently so that the sights are not in your line of sight and you can see the threat clearly. This is certainly not a safety violation. Remember that the subject of your attention is acting or has acted in a manner sufficiently dangerous to cause you grave enough concern to bring a weapon out. This is doubly true if confronting a house breaker since you both know he does not belong there!

Cover is critical. You can easily generalize that, in a face-to-face encounter, the one who moves first may be the one who wins. This holds true until you interject such variables as surprise, cover, distance, and darkness. Attention to these details will impede the aggressor's ability to react to your presence and can minimize your exposure to his gunfire.

Exactly what do you say to the man in your sights? Before selecting your prose, let's consider the following. Talking and shooting at the same time is *very difficult!* You should not try to open up a dialogue with the thug. Not only will this be distracting, but most crooks are poor conversationalists. If he does begin to talk, order him to be silent. If he persists, you can't simply shoot him, but you are ready for the move he's trying to conceal with his words.

Avoid using empty threats or colorful gutter language. Strong voice and command presence will do more for you than foul words. Some instructors advocate being "vague." They suggest phrases like "I'll take appropriate action" instead of just telling him you'll kill him. I disagree. Being vague requires the use of too many words. I have seen many people held at gunpoint and contend that you will get much more compliance by being clear and forceful.

Keep the words short and simple, with hard consonants and few syllables. Make use of forceful orders, not wimpy requests. It is not, "hold it?" it is, "HOLD IT!" Other good commands are "STOP!" "DON'T MOVE!" and "HALT!"

Do not use a command ordering movement at first. If you do, the thug will probably feign initial compliance, only to take an aggressive posture while you wait for him to obey your orders.

Consider the fact that English may not be the predominant language in some urban areas. A master's degree in linguistics is not necessary, but a few properly memorized words and phrases in the appropriate language might be useful.

The next step is to disarm the aggressor if there is any weapon in evidence. It would be best to do this from behind, but sometimes we cannot choose our positions. If he has a gun in his belt or elsewhere, you'd better not let him go near it. If he has a gun in his hands, order him to drop it at once. Some believe that it is best to order the suspect to *slowly* place the gun down instead of dropping it for fear of it discharging on impact. This is a real concern, but the longer the adversary has control of his weapon, the longer you are in danger (remember reaction times). Order him to drop it and minimize your risk before anything else. If he is facing you with the gun in his hand, you have a different situation—shoot him at once.

When the weapon is on the ground, have him step away from it. Now order him to face away from you. If he does not comply with your orders, the situation has changed and you will have an important decision to make.

Once he is turned away, order him to raise his hands with his arms straight up. It is the hands that can kill—watch them! The final step is to secure him. This may mean handcuffs or simply placing him in an awkward prone position that will be difficult for him to move out of. Your partner—if you have one—can move in and handcuff him or, in the case of a lone citizen, you can call the police. Where is the phone? Can you reach it without exposing yourself? Think about these things beforehand!

If calling the police is the course of action, be careful of what you say. You'd better not forget to tell them that you are armed and holding a prisoner at gunpoint. Give the dispatcher a good description of yourself and then of your captive. This will help prevent terminal confusion when the "blue suits" arrive.

How will you let the police in to take custody of the prisoner? Let's figure that one out now, not later! When the police do arrive, it is important to be discreet with your weapon. This means reholstering or at least securing it in the waistband of your trousers. It is not wise to greet a group of nervous cops while waving a pistol about. I was once greeted by a victimized homeowner who'd armed herself for fear that a burglar would return. I was coolheaded. Don't bet that the officers who respond to your call will be.

Here is another consideration: when you challenge the intruder, he may flee. Whether you shoot him or not is a personal decision. The choice will greatly depend on your rules of engagement, the local laws, and the particulars of your situation. It may not be acceptable, for example, to shoot a young gang member who is making off with your car stereo. On the other hand, the same subject fleeing from your dark and open doorway some late night as you pull into your driveway may be a very different situation indeed, especially if the status of family members within is unknown.

Study the laws in your particular area and take notice of your home environment and possible situations in which you would most likely have to fight. You must keep these things strongly in mind while developing a good tactical plan, and then follow it when you hear something that goes "bump" in the night!

Tactical Considerations in Vehicles

Once a nation of horsemen, we are now a nation of motorists. Most of us spend a good deal of our time in and around automobiles. So do criminals. Carjacking has almost become a casual pastime for many of our young urban terrorists. Therefore it is important to examine your options if you become embattled while behind the wheel.

Clearly the primary mission of an automobile in a tactical situation is as a means of escape from the area. If you are ensconced in the driver seat when you see trouble coming, it is a simple thing to drive away from it. The important thing is to realize that tactically evading trouble supersedes the rules of the road. I recall a conversation with a victim of the infamous Los Angeles riots of 1992. This man had stopped for a red light at the notorious intersection of Florence and Normandie when his vehicle was rushed by a horde of street ruffians. The motorist was subsequently dragged from his vehicle and beaten severely. Having barely escaped with his life, he was asked why he didn't simply drive away? His honest answer was that he could not drive through a red light!

Once your escape is made, you must be alert for pursuers.

If you are being pursued, driving right up onto the lawn of the local police station might be one option. If this isn't possible, a second option might be to drive to a position of cover, quickly exit the vehicle, and then wait for your tormentors to arrive. When they do, shoot them as they approach your car.

If you cannot drive away, plan B is to put the wheels to your attackers and run them over flat! The stopping power of an automobile is substantially greater than that of even the most powerful handgun. Use it. This is also an option if your adversaries are attempting to block you in with their own vehicles while they close the distance.

Cultivating a proper mind-set is crucial while driving because it is very easy to "drift off" mentally in the enclosed, climate-controlled, stereophonic interior of a vehicle. Look around and notice the other cars around you and who is inside them, particularly at traffic lights. Note any vehicles that keep a constant distance behind you as you vary your speed and route. If such vehicles contain suspicious characters, pay greater attention to them. Most times nothing will happen, but you must be ready if it ever does.

Many citizens, choosing not to be victimized, carry firearms for protection in their cars. Consider that the popular strong-side hip holster may be difficult to draw from in the seated and belted position that driving requires. Many associates of mine remove the pistol from their strong-side holster and tuck it in their waist at the appendix or in the crossdraw position for better access. These positions are much more efficient for seated presentations. (Those spending a majority of time seated should take note.)

Another option is to carry a second pistol and place it in an easy-to-reach position inside the car. Other options include the shoulder holster or a second pistol in an ankle rig. One method that is not recommended except for a second pistol is carrying it under the strong-side thigh as you sit in the driver's seat. An FBI agent in the infamous Miami shoot-out tried that. An unexpected collision dislodged the pistol completely, disarming the agent prior to the ensuing gun battle. Realize that driving and shooting is not a good idea. You should do one or the other.

If both escape and justifiable vehicular homicide are ruled out as viable options, your only alternative is the pistol. Only in extremely unusual situations will you shoot at an adversary while still seated in the car. Such situations might arise if you are attacked while stuck in traffic, at the drive-through window of a fast food restaurant, or simply parked waiting for a loved one. Such surprise scenarios will require initial responses while seated followed by either exiting the vehicle or driving away. This is not difficult when you realize that in most cases the criminal will not just "open fire" on your car by surprise but rather will attempt to extract you at gunpoint to commandeer your vehicle. There are only two locations from which he can successfully do this: the driver's door and the passenger's door. To react, you must develop a seated response to each direction.

The draw and response to the left is preceded by a forward lean toward the steering wheel to allow the strong hand a proper grip on the pistol. (This move is unnecessary for the crossdraw or appendix position users.) Once the pistol is in hand, push on the floorboard with your left foot and drop your shoulders toward the passenger side door. As you drop back, raise the pistol and begin shooting the adversary at the driver's door.

To respond to the passenger side assault, precede the

draw with the same motion and lean your shoulders toward the driver side door as you complete a one-handed draw toward the passenger side. The restrictive sitting position coupled with average torso flexibility prevents a two-handed hold. Note that these are specialized techniques for specialized circumstances. If you can exit the car without incurring extraordinary risks, do so.

If you are going to exit the car, how will you deal with the seat belt? Personally, I do not wear them while driving in the city. I've heard all the stories about how they save lives, but I consider it a balance of risk between a crash and a shooting situation. We must all decide that one for ourselves.

Having a second pistol in the car and almost in hand is the easiest presentation. Drawing from a strong-side hip holster while exiting a vehicle is not difficult, but it must be practiced. First, dip the shoulders forward as before to allow the hand to get to the pistol. Simultaneously, the strong hand moves to grip the pistol while the support hand actuates the door lever. The support-side leg pushes the door open and holds it in place as you exit. The pistol should be drawn in a smooth motion as you exit the car.

Once outside, you can use the car itself for cover. Except for the windows, automobiles are remarkably resistant to gunfire, particularly the engine block area.

One of your most vulnerable times will be when you are either entering or exiting the car. Most carjackings occur then. This is where a proper combat mind-set is paramount. Examine the surroundings for questionable people before committing yourself to entry or exit. Often, just being aware of their presence is enough.

When in a car, your initial plan should be to drive away if possible, drive over them if necessary, and shoot only as a last resort. If you can exit the vehicle prior to shooting, do so, but if that is not tactically possible, then you must respond from where you sit. Tactical situations involving automobiles have their own set of peculiarities, and you should study them to prepare for those unexpected "road hazards."

The Undiscovered Country

The past few years have seen great strides in the fields of weapons development and training. Never before in modern history have so many people been interested and involved in owning, carrying, and learning to use weapons.

One reason for this fascination is, of course, a concern over the prevalence of criminals in our society. The other reason is the concern that an increasingly paternalistic government will continue to restrict, and eventually try to prevent, the ownership of arms by private citizens. This is a very valid concern because historically, without weapons, the rights of the people exist only at the whim of the governing body. Without the routine ownership of weapons by private citizens, the Bill of Rights is only a worthless scrap of paper. The issue is not the freedom to own guns but the existence of freedom itself!

There is a sick notion in our country to sacrifice our personal liberty in order to promote a "safe and stable" society. The idiocy of this idea is easily seen when you realize that no law can ever prevent an individual from committing a crime—it can only punish him after the act. Crime is a matter of will that cannot be controlled by legislation. This same legislation can, however, affect and incrementally strip away the rights of law-abiding citizens.

You cannot affect the prevalence of criminals very much because there have always been evil men, and that is not likely to change as long as man walks on this earth. But you can affect and prevent the erosion of freedom by joining the National Rifle Association, voting, and becoming involved in the political process. Gun ownership, freedom, and political involvement are interdependent on each other. The future of these, as well as the future of our country, is in *our* hands.

I believe that we can undo the damage already done, restore the importance of the Second Amendment, and preserve our freedom into the "undiscovered country" that is the future in the coming century.

Selected Bibliography

California P.O.S.T.: *Violence Against California Peace Officers*, California Commission P.O.S.T., 1994.

Cooper, Jeff: *Another Country*, Gunsite Press, 1992.
— *Cooper on Handguns*, Petersen Publications, 1979.
— *Fireworks*, Gunsite Press, 1990.
— *Principles of Personal Defense*, Paladin Press, 1979.
— *To Ride, Shoot Straight, and Speak the Truth*, Gunsite Press, 1988.

FBI Uniform Crime Report, 1983-1993.

Garfield, Charles A.: *Peak Performance*, Warner Books, 1984.

Griffin, Samuel B.: *Sun Tzu—The Art of War*, Oxford University Press, 1963.

Jordan, Bill: *No Second Place Winner*, W.H. Jordan, 1965.

LaPierre, Wayne: *Guns, Crime, and Freedom*, Regnery Publishing Inc., 1994.

Loehr, James E.: *Mental Toughness Training for Sports*, Penguin Books, 1982.

Millman, Dan: *The Warrior Athlete*, Stillpoint Publishing, 1979.

Morrison, Gregory B.: *The Modern Technique of the Pistol*, Gunsite Press, 1991.

Musashi, Miyamoto: *A Book of Five Rings*, Overlook Press, 1974.

Plaxco, Michael: *Shooting from Within*, Zediker Publishing, 1991.

Remsberg, Charles: *Street Survival*, Calibre Press, 1980.
— *The Tactical Edge*, Calibre Press, 1986.

Rosa, Joseph G.: *The Gunfighter, Man or Myth?*, University of Oklahoma Press, 1969.

Taylor, Chuck: *The Complete Book of Combat Handgunning*, Desert Publications, 1982.